Praise for
An Introduction to Christian
Philosophical Theology

The practice of Christian philosophical theology—the application of philosophy to the challenging questions raised by Christian doctrines—is almost as old as the church. Yet only in the last half century has it emerged as a distinctive scholarly discipline. While a truly impressive amount of work has been produced in recent decades, few good resources are available to orient students and nonspecialists to this important and exciting field. This fine volume helps fill that lacuna. Stephen T. Davis and Eric T. Yang have written an accessible and admirably even-handed survey of the state of the art in Christian philosophical theology. It is not only a reliable introduction covering a wide range of topics but also an enthusiastic invitation to join the ongoing conversation and participate in the perennial task of "faith seeking understanding."

—**JAMES N. ANDERSON,** Carl W. McMurray
Professor of Theology and Philosophy,
Reformed Theological Seminary, Charlotte

Thinking deeply and clearly about God is imperative for all Christians. The task of theology brings biblical, historical, and systematic resources to bear on the fundamental questions of Christianity. Davis and Yang ensure that the philosophical remains in the theologian's toolbox. This text offers a winsome and accessible foray into philosophically sophisticated discussions of core Christian doctrines. It is grounded in traditional discussions of these issues but focuses on state-of-the-art engagements with contemporary philosophical treatments. This text will be a helpful accompaniment for students, pastors, and scholars as they think through central topics of Christian theology.

—**JAMES M. ACARDI,** assistant professor
of biblical and systematic theology,
Trinity Evangelical Divinity School

I've been waiting for a book like this for a long time. Although others have written on the relationship between philosophy and theology, none do so with such clarity and accessibility, making this an excellent tool for anyone seeking to understand how philosophy can be a resource for theological reflection. Tackling a range of difficult theological issues, Yang and Davis somehow manage to model both critical acumen and charitable engagement, consistently helping the reader appreciate the complexity of the conversation without overwhelming detail or unnecessarily technical jargon. If you've ever wondered what Athens has to do with Jerusalem, this would be a great place to start.

—MARC CORTEZ, professor of
theology, Wheaton College

Here, two exacting philosophers, with extensive ministry experience, take up long-standing questions about important Christian beliefs. Shaking off what the academy expects of "professional philosophers," Davis and Yang steer a course within the coordinates of Scripture and the historic Christian faith. Christianity cannot be taken seriously without deep reflection on the meaning of its central doctrines and the evidential support they enjoy. The authors, therefore, explore key questions that cluster around issues of ultimate concern, for believers and nonbelievers alike. And they do so with that unusual balance of intellectual rigor, readability, and pastoral care.

—R. DOUGLAS GEIVETT, professor of philosophy,
Talbot Department of Philosophy, Biola University

In an anti-intellectual and sound-bite age, serious thinking on key Christian doctrines is needed. Stephen Davis and Eric Yang's *An Introduction to Christian Philosophical Theology* is the book I've been waiting for! Accessibly written, historically informed, and conversant with the contemporary discussion, Davis and Yang's book powerfully demonstrates the coherence, intelligibility, and beauty of key Christian doctrines. You will be challenged intellectually and nourished spiritually. I highly recommend this book to theology and philosophy students—indeed, to any Christian seeking to better understand the deep truths of the Christian faith.

—PAUL M. GOULD, associate professor of philosophy
of religion and director of the MA in Philosophy of
Religion Program, Palm Beach Atlantic University

In an accessible and engaging text for those new to contemporary Christian philosophical theology in the analytic tradition, Davis and Yang illustrate how philosophical tools and concepts can faithfully serve the Christian faith seeking understanding project alongside of—and not in tension with—biblical, systematic, and historical theologians. They capably guide the reader through the terrain of analytic Christian philosophical theology, both the well-worn paths as well as new vistas on the cutting edge of contemporary discussion in the areas of Scripture, Trinity, incarnation, atonement, and personal eschatology (bodily resurrection and the final state). Davis and Yang are to be commended for carrying out their task in a spirit of faithful stewardship to the church and a humble dependence on Scripture and the wider consensual Christian tradition. It is a sorely needed book that fills a sizable gap in the literature and will serve seminary and divinity students well. Rightly ordered thinking about God and all things in relation to God takes a great deal of human grit and divine grace; Davis and Yang have provided students an excellent place to begin.

—**ROSS D. INMAN,** associate professor of philosophy, Southeastern Baptist Theological Seminary, editor of *Philosophia Christi.*

Though philosophical theology has a rich and historic pedigree, comparatively few Christians today are acquainted with its insights and contributions to understanding difficult theological topics. Davis and Yang thoughtfully and capably introduce newcomers to philosophical theology by showing how to ask and explore answers to philosophical questions about core Christian beliefs. Seminary and undergraduate students, as well as church leaders, will find in these pages accessible but nevertheless penetrating discussions that take seriously the claims of Scripture and are well informed by contemporary scholarship. I highly recommend *An Introduction to Christian Philosophical Theology* as a wonderful primer on philosophical theology.

—**R. KEITH LOFTIN,** associate professor of philosophy and humanities, Scarborough College

This wonderful book by Eric T. Yang and Stephen T. Davis offers a contemporary introduction to philosophical theology, and it ably demonstrates the relevance and importance of philosophy for theology. It addresses questions that are not only significant and complicated but also quite common, and it does so with sparkling clarity, deep insight, and overall winsomeness. It will be a blessing not only to students and scholars but also to pastors and preachers. I recommend it highly, and I plan to return to it often.

—**THOMAS MCCALL,** professor of theology
and scholar in residence, Asbury University

An Introduction to Christian Philosophical Theology is a thorough, biblical, and interesting guide for thinking philosophically about key theological issues. This book is ideal for pastors, students, and thoughtful Christians who want to go deeper in their understanding of theological issues as diverse as the nature of Scripture, the Trinity, and the afterlife. You don't have to have a background in philosophy or theology to appreciate this text because Davis and Yang explain key concepts along the way. But even if you do, you will nevertheless find many helpful insights and clarifications along the way. This is a superb text that I am honored to endorse.

—**SEAN MCDOWELL,** associate professor of Christian
apologetics, Talbot School of Theology, Biola University

An Introduction to Christian Philosophical Theology is as delightful as it is important. While first-rate philosophers, Davis and Yang have managed to write this crucial book with creativity, clarity, and a readable, engaging style. Their book is accessible to a general reader without being simplistic or watered down. Perhaps more important is the range of topics they cover. They are just the right ones for a book like this. Let's be honest. There is a crying need among Christians to learn how to think carefully and deeply about their faith. Where does one go to learn how to do this? Look no further. Because it combines accessibility with deep, careful reflection, I envision *An Introduction to Christian Philosophical Theology* becoming *the* go-to book to meet this need.

—**J. P. MORELAND,** distinguished professor
of philosophy, Talbot School of Theology, Biola
University, author of *Scientism and Secularism*

Davis and Yang have produced an admirably concise and clear introduction to the fascinating field of contemporary philosophical theology. Students will appreciate the book's simplicity and find themselves captivated by some of the creative ways philosophical theologians address perennial questions about such topics as the Trinity, deity of Christ, resurrection, heaven and hell. Davis and Yang have also managed to produce a reliable introduction useful to biblical scholars and systematic theologians who sense there is a great deal to learn from the renaissance of Christian philosophy but may find the literature daunting. On debated issues, Davis and Yang state their preferences but also suggest ways in which students and professors inclined toward other positions may defend and develop them. *An Introduction to Christian Philosophical Theology* is a model of intellectual charity, a virtue too often in short supply.

—CARL MOSSER, New Testament
scholar and theologian

This book is a beginner-friendly—but not dumbed-down—exploration into the main topics of Christian philosophical theology. The authors represent the current state of the debates faithfully and in a manner that both engages the reader and invites the reader to further reflection. I recommend this book both to the beginner and to the scholar who wants a fair and broad representation of the discussions in Christian philosophical theology.

—TIM PAWL, professor of philosophy,
University of St. Thomas

One question I always had in church about Christian doctrine was, "But why do we believe that?" What I found was that the church was lacking in training on the philosophical understanding of the basic doctrines being taught. Davis and Yang present a uniquely powerful introduction to this much-needed field of Christian education in a truly accessible and fair manner. This book fills a glaring gap in discipleship, and yet it does so with a humble approach that makes learning enjoyable. I not only recommend this work for university or seminary students but also highly recommend it as a study in the local church.

—MARY JO SHARP, assistant professor of
apologetics, Houston Baptist University

A theology that lacks conceptual clarity will fail in its task of providing guidance to ecclesial praxis. *An Introduction to Christian Philosophical Theology* is set to be a popular resource for anyone interested in probing the philosophical agility of Christian doctrine. While the faith of Christians remains mysterious since it adores a transcendent God who became man, it seeks an understanding that respects reason and logic. Davis and Yang are knowledgeable yet patient guides to those who have taken up this quest.

—**ADONIS VIDU,** professor of theology,
Gordon-Conwell Theological Seminary

Davis and Yang have produced an introduction to the field of philosophical theology that is remarkably informative as well as concise and to the point. Each chapter provides a focused analysis of the issues at stake and the major options that are on the table. This is the ideal text to initiate students into this vitally important and existentially engaging conversation.

—**JERRY L. WALLS,** professor of philosophy and
scholar in residence, Houston Baptist University

This excellent introduction to philosophical theology combines philosophical sophistication with accessibility to nonphilosophers. Written in a lively, personable style, it will be a welcome addition to the education of ministers, church leaders, and any Christian interested in the philosophical issues arising from their faith.

—**LINDA ZAGZEBSKI,** George Lynn Cross Research
Professor and Kingfisher College Chair of the Philosophy
of Religion and Ethics, University of Oklahoma

AN INTRODUCTION TO

CHRISTIAN PHILOSOPHICAL THEOLOGY

FAITH SEEKING UNDERSTANDING

STEPHEN T. DAVIS
& ERIC T. YANG

ZONDERVAN ACADEMIC

An Introduction to Christian Philosophical Theology
Copyright © 2020 by Stephen T. Davis and Eric T. Yang

Requests for information should be addressed to:
Zondervan, *3900 Sparks Dr. SE, Grand Rapids, Michigan 49546*

Zondervan titles may be purchased in bulk for educational, business, fundraising, or sales promotional use. For information, please email SpecialMarkets@Zondervan.com.

ISBN 978-0-310-10408-7 (softcover)

ISBN 978-0-310-12037-7 (audio)

ISBN 978-0-310-10409-4 (ebook)

Cover design: Kristen Andrews
Cover photo: © Slanapotam / Shutterstock
Interior design: Kait Lamphere

Printed in the United States of America

20 21 22 23 24 25 26 27 28 29 30 /LSC/ 15 14 13 12 11 10 9 8 7 6 5 4 3 2 1

To Mom and Dad, Sue and Peter Yang,
who have taught me by their words and shown
me in their lives that there is no project more
worthwhile than loving God and loving others

—ERIC

To my sons, Adam Christopher Davis
and Nathan Andrew Davis

—STEVE

CONTENTS

INTRODUCTION

Theology involves thinking and speaking about God, which is a task that should be approached with some measure of fear and trembling. Theology matters not just in academia or in the classroom but also in the everyday lives of Christians who worship God and believe in him. One reason why it matters a great deal is that it can help people avoid theological errors about Christian doctrines. Thinking and speaking about God is a daunting task, and the risk of slipping into serious error is always a possibility when doing theology.

For example, when discussing the doctrine of the Trinity, it is quite easy to end up saying things that would explicitly or implicitly espouse modalism (that the Godhead is only one person who plays different roles) or tritheism (that there are three Gods). When preaching a sermon on the Trinity, one has to be extremely careful not to say something contradictory or heretical. No doubt traditional Christians will desire to avoid stating anything heretical, but the risk is there—and we believe the risk is increased if one fails to understand the complex issues and concepts that are involved in some of these doctrines. Failure to be precise and attentive to such complexities can lead to saying something logically inconsistent or incomprehensible. Nor does it help to try and avoid doing theology. Those who attempt to avoid doing theology usually don't—rather, they end up with a poor theology.

Thus, having a good grasp of theology is crucial, especially for those who are church leaders or training to become leaders. We hope that this book can serve as a useful resource for those who are trying to understand the logical and philosophical questions concerning specific Christian doctrines. Although we, the authors, are professional academics whose primary work has been in a university setting, both of us have also served in church ministry. One of us (Davis) has been an ordained minister in a Reformed denomination for many decades, and the other (Yang) has served as a youth, college, young adult, and worship pastor for more than a decade. We have been uniquely fortunate to have a foot in both the life of the university and the life of the church, and we hope our experience can help bridge the two.

We believe that training in logic or philosophy is important for future theologians and church leaders. If you are a church leader, pastor, or seminarian, you have probably studied systematic theology, biblical exegesis, historical theology, and so forth. Additionally, many pastors and seminary students are receiving training in apologetics and philosophy of religion. Christian apologetics provides reasons for one's beliefs as well as responds to objections to or criticisms of Christianity. Philosophy of religion is a domain in philosophy that focuses on several philosophical questions or issues related to religion in general or to a specific religion, such as Christianity, Judaism, or Islam. Typical topics in philosophy of religion focus on arguments for and against God's existence (and so there is often overlap with apologetics) and questions about God's attributes, in particular what attributes God has and how best to analyze them. For example, philosophers of religion ask whether God is simple, immutable, or timeless (and how best to understand those attributes), and they also try to provide an analysis of less contentious divine attributes, such as omnipotence, omniscience, divine goodness, and the like. They also focus on questions related to religious language, the epistemology of religious beliefs (that is, how we can acquire religious knowledge), and the diversity of religions. Many of these questions are not religion-specific, and many of the claims discussed in philosophy of religion are defended through argument.

Even for those without seminary or academic training, ample resources are available for learning some of the basics in apologetics and philosophy of religion. For example, in apologetics, we would commend (among many other books) William Lane Craig's *On Guard* and *Reasonable Faith*, Peter Kreeft and Ronald Tacelli's *Handbook of Christian Apologetics*, Alister McGrath's *Mere Apologetics*, and the recently published *Rational Faith*, written by one of us (Davis). Many introductory textbooks and anthologies in philosophy of religion are also available, as well as an array of videos, websites, and podcasts that address these topics.

Nevertheless, we have found many Christians, including pastors and seminary students, untrained in *philosophical theology*. We will say more about what philosophical theology is in chapter 1, but in brief it involves employing philosophical tools while studying topics in Christian theology. Often little training is offered in examining the logical consistency or intelligibility of the key doctrines of the Christian faith, such as the doctrine of the Trinity or the incarnation. We have even heard someone say that the doctrine of the Trinity requires that Christians believe that three equals one $(3 = 1)$, which should make any mathematician cringe!

Although several books and articles on philosophical theology have been written, many of them are not comprehensible to those without the requisite training in philosophy. So we have written this book as a user-friendly guide for those interested in asking philosophical questions about the Trinity, the incarnation, the atonement, the resurrection, and other Christian doctrines. We will show what sort of contribution philosophical reasoning can bring while studying and reflecting on some of the core Christian doctrines, and we sincerely hope that this book serves as a helpful introduction to these issues and ideas.

We expect this book to be used in a classroom setting, in an undergraduate or graduate course; and we would recommend pairing the chapters with some of the articles or books that are suggested in the Further Readings section at the end of each chapter. The chapters have been written to stand on their own, and so chapters may be read in any order (though the book's structure follows the typical conceptual ordering found in many theology books).

However, we tried to write the book so that readers outside of academia can benefit from it as well. Our desire is that this book will be useful to pastors, church leaders, small group leaders, and interested readers who want to reflect more deeply on some of these enduring questions concerning Christian beliefs. The study of philosophical theology can broaden and deepen your understanding of central Christian doctrines, and it can help you avoid egregious errors—some of which have even been condemned as heresies in church history. Our goal for this book is for it to spark further reflection that can transform the thought and practice of those committed to following the way of Jesus Christ.

This book does not delve deeply into the history or historical development of these doctrines; this is in part because several great introductory books in historical theology that discuss the historical development of Christian doctrines are already available. Also, several issues discussed in this book overlap some of what can be learned in systematic theology. This book is not meant to replace such works; it is meant to fill in the gap between philosophical and analytic theorizing of difficult Christian teachings to ensure that what one believes is logically consistent, coherent, and intelligible. These philosophical virtues are not the only things that matter when it comes to doctrine and faith. Christians must above all continue to study Scripture and pray as we thoughtfully reflect on these topics.

As you will discover, much disagreement and intramural debate exists among Christian philosophical theologians. We will try our best to present different views as fairly as we can, though in some of the chapters, we will defend our own favored views as well as present criticisms or concerns with various accounts (though it is the case that we, the authors, do not even agree with each other on several of these issues!). We do hope that readers will assess and evaluate each view on its own merits. What you may notice is that there is often no one mandatory way to understand a particular Christian doctrine. Most of these doctrines are mysteries, so it is no surprise that we will not fully understand them. And we do not ever expect to fully understand them, especially in this life.

When faced with these difficult issues, one may be tempted to say that they are so mysterious that we are unable to have any coherent understanding of them at all. Usually this becomes a conversation stopper, which is quite unfortunate. After all, what Scripture and theologians have typically meant by "mystery" is the revealing of something not previously known and something that could not have been known without divine revelation. Saying "we can't ever understand" in response to difficult doctrines may lead to intellectual laziness or sloppy thinking. Of course, no sensible Christian would claim that we could ever completely understand these Christian doctrines. But Christians have a responsibility to present a logically consistent account of Christian doctrines; for we reject certain religions or certain claims from other religions on the grounds that they are logically inconsistent or unintelligible. So, at a bare minimum, Christian doctrines should not contain logical contradictions or be utterly incomprehensible.

To be clear, our goal is not to solve these theological quandaries the way we solve puzzles and riddles. Rather, the goal is to deepen our understanding and appreciation of doctrines we believe because God has revealed them to us. For much of the Christian intellectual tradition, there has been reference to the following motto: *faith seeking understanding*. In step with traditional Christian thought, we, too, adhere to that motto.

Let us explain what we mean by the motto. We, the authors, fully embrace the core tenets of traditional Christianity. We believe in the triune God (Father, Son, and Spirit), who has created and continues to sustain the world. This God has spoken (and is speaking) to us through the Bible, which is authoritative in matters pertaining to faith and practice. Because of the rebellion and sin of human beings, human beings have been separated from God. But God, in his grace and love, enacted a rescue plan culminating in the person of Jesus Christ, who is both truly God and truly man. Through Jesus's life, death, and resurrection, we have been redeemed and reconciled to God. Jesus will one day return, and from the moment of the resurrection of the dead, the blessed will live with him forevermore.

There is more to this that we regard as essential to Christianity. But even from these beliefs, many questions naturally arise:

- How can there be one God if there are three persons, each of whom is God?
- How can someone be God and human at the same time—doesn't that mean that Jesus is omnipotent and not omnipotent at the same time, and how is that possible?
- How does God reconcile himself to us—does he have to pay off the devil, or does he pay some penalty or make some sort of compensation?
- How does God deliver his message to us, and how is the Bible an inspired book?
- If we are supposed to be resurrected after we die, how can our bodies be resurrected if we've been cremated or vaporized?

So we are people who begin with faith. But once we start thinking about and reflecting on what we believe, a whole host of questions arise, and hence we have a faith that seeks understanding. Though we will never fully understand the mystery of God and his ways, we want to know as much as we can, just as lovers want to know as much as they can about their beloved. Lovers ask questions. If you love a sport or a particular team, then you will want to find out quite a lot about it. If you love a person, then you will want to know the details of their personality and their history. If Christians are to love God with their whole hearts, souls, minds, and strength (Mark 12:30), then how much more should you want to know and understand all that you can know and understand about him? For us, the authors, our love for God is what motivated our academic and intellectual pursuits. And we are inviting you to join us. We can say from experience that our philosophical and theological reflections on these issues have not gotten in the way of our worship of God; instead, they have increased our awe and love for the God who has revealed himself to us.

You may have heard the oft-repeated joke about the theologian who died, and when given an offer to go either to heaven or to a lecture on heaven, he chose to go to the lecture. Anything that is good and is not God can get in the way of our worship of God, be it food, human relationships, sports, academic promotions, and the like (and we have been tempted to idolatry by some of these things—Lord, forgive us!). But that does not mean we should get rid of those things; it just means we should be cautious and not forget the ultimate goal, which is to love the Lord our God with all our heart, soul, mind, and strength (Mark 12:30). So we do not think that serious, careful, and logical reflection on Christian doctrine should be abandoned merely because it leaves open the possibility of losing sight of our ultimate goal. We would be the first to say that praying to God is far more important than reading this book.

We hope that you will find that philosophers have something to contribute to our attempt to think and speak about God. But philosophers have much to learn from systematic theologians, historical theologians, biblical exegetes, and all other Christians who have an interactive relationship with God. As two Christian academics and philosophers, we offer this book as our very small contribution to the task of doing theology together across the disciplines and across the church—to the greater glory of God!

We are grateful to our friends both in academia and in church ministry who have inspired us to write this book and have helped us through many conversations about the topics covered herein. Josh Camacho,

David Frederick, and Rev. Jonathan Hughes offered helpful comments on a few of the chapters as well as encouragement as we worked on the manuscript. We would like to offer our special thanks to Br. John Baptist Santa Ana, OSB, Joseph Jedwab, Nat Tabris, David Vosburg, and Alissa Yang for reading the entirety of an earlier version of this manuscript and offering us many helpful comments and suggestions. We are especially indebted to our editor, Katya Covrett, for her assistance and encouragement, without which this book would not have seen the light of day.

Each chapter should be seen as the collaborative effort of both authors. But for full disclosure, Stephen T. Davis was the principal author of chapters 1, 2, and 5, and Eric T. Yang was the principal author of chapters 3, 4, 6, and 7.

PHILOSOPHICAL THEOLOGY

What Is It? Why Do We Need It?

1

This book is about philosophical theology. We intend to explain what it is and why it is a valuable endeavor. But before doing that, we first need to clarify some terms. We will look first at *theology*, then *philosophy*, and finally *philosophical theology*.

WHAT IS THEOLOGY?

Theology can be characterized as *the attempt to think clearly and methodically about the doctrines that Christians believe were revealed to us by God.* Many of those doctrines are obviously essential to Christianity. They include beliefs about God, Christ, the world, human beings, the future, and many other things. Theology is an attempt to clarify and explain what those doctrines are. We would argue that theology is something every Christian practices, but there are also many recognized theologians in the church, both past and present. Obviously, Christians do not always agree on doctrine; theology is often argumentative. But we would also claim that there are certain core beliefs that are essential to Christianity and that all Christians should hold.[1] We will discuss several of these core beliefs.

There are many branches of theology. *Systematic theology* attempts to say what Christian doctrines are and how they hang together to

---

1. In this book we will take "Christianity" (and its cognates) to refer to what C. S. Lewis called "mere Christianity" in his well-known book by the same name.

form a coherent whole. *Biblical theology* endeavors to clarify and explain the beliefs, practices, and concepts taught in the Bible. *Historical theology* investigates and explains the work of past theologians and the teachings of the classic creeds. *Natural theology* is the attempt to prove particular Christian beliefs by the use of human reason alone, apart from special revelation, such as the existence of God or God's attributes. *Moral theology* seeks to express biblical and Christian teachings about what is right and wrong, about what duties and obligations there are—both for individuals and societies. *Pastoral theology* applies Christian teaching to the practical tasks of helping people live, especially in their everyday experiences, which includes dealing with suffering. *Apologetics* is the task of defending Christian beliefs, both by presenting arguments in favor of them and by defending them against criticisms.[2]

WHAT IS PHILOSOPHY?

Philosophers notoriously disagree about how to define the word *philosophy* (although, interestingly, there is broad agreement on who the great philosophers were and what problems philosophers discuss). As we understand it, philosophy involves *the attempt to answer ultimate questions*. An ultimate question is a question that (1) people are deeply interested in and desperately long to answer, and that (2) cannot be answered by the methods of science. The question "Was Julius Caesar right-handed or left-handed?" is not a philosophical question because nobody is deeply interested in it. It is hard to imagine anybody spending three hours thinking hard about it. The question "Is there life on Mars?" *is* a question that people are very much interested in answering,

---

2. We recognize that disagreements exist over how to characterize these disciplines, and we are fully aware that some people may not approve of our characterization of these branches of theology. While we think oversimplifications should generally be avoided, since our main task is not providing an accurate characterization of other branches of theology, we believe this broad overview is acceptable for our purposes.

but it can be answered by science, and no doubt one day will be. So this question is not a philosophical question either.

Well, then, what are some ultimate questions? Here are a few:

- Will I live on after I die?
- What makes me the same person over time?
- What is knowledge, and how does it differ from other cognitive states like belief or opinion?
- Can I know I am not dreaming or in a computer simulation?
- What is the meaning of life?
- Who is living the good life?
- What makes an action right or wrong?
- Does God exist?
- Can my actions be both free and determined?

These are questions that keep reappearing in the history of human thought (and keep some people up at night!), and they do not seem to be answerable by the methods of science. We cannot conduct an experiment, crunch numbers, or take a poll to find the answers. They are, then, ultimate questions.

Philosophy seems to some people to be vague, speculative, and irrelevant to real life. But it should not be so. Philosophy tries to help people in a concrete way: it tries to answer questions like these that fascinate many of us. Philosophy is not just for professional philosophers. Anyone who asks an ultimate question is a philosopher. We encounter philosophical questions in unexpected places—not just in the classroom but also in the marketplace, not just in dusty textbooks but also in movies, songs, novels, and poems.

Philosophy can be both fascinating and frustrating. The fascination emerges from the intrinsically interesting questions it considers. The frustration emerges from the fact that philosophical investigations do not always yield clear or easy answers. Often the end result of philosophical inquiry is more questions. This was the case for the Greek philosopher Socrates, and it made his interlocutors quite upset! Even if we cannot satisfactorily answer every philosophical question, we think progress is made when the questions we care about are further clarified, when certain positions are ruled out, and when we get a better handle on what approach or which method would be useful in addressing certain questions.

The limitation of philosophical inquiry is not necessarily a defect—and why there is such an intellectual limitation is even a philosophical question. But we think that recognition of such limitations can produce intellectual humility, and we believe that the practice of philosophy can help inculcate other intellectual virtues as well, such as open-mindedness, intellectual autonomy, intellectual carefulness, and the like. So even if you do not walk away with answers to some of the ultimate questions, practicing philosophy or engaging in philosophical inquiry can help you become a more intellectually virtuous person.

That said, we do think that we can answer some ultimate questions, even if we aren't certain of our answers or even if disagreement with other philosophers remains. We even think that we have found some answers to some of the ultimate questions, though we recognize our fallibility, which is why we want to continue engaging in discussion. Being certain about anything is hard, and so philosophers typically welcome objections and criticisms to their views and arguments, since being shown where we went wrong would be an intellectual improvement. The goal of argumentation, as we see it, is not to be combative; rather, it is a way of offering reasons for one's views or of raising concerns with various attempts to answer ultimate questions.

PHILOSOPHY AND CHRISTIAN THEOLOGY

Before we move on to explaining what philosophical theology is, we should ask what the relationship is between philosophy and Christian theology. This is a complicated question. On the one hand, it is clear that there are similarities between the two. Many of the questions asked by philosophers are similar to those that theologians attempt to answer: Does God exist? What will happen to me when I die? What is the meaning of life? Also, philosophers and theologians share certain methodological preferences: both strive for connected, systematic thinking. Moreover, both disciplines are to an extent backward-looking disciplines. Both philosophers and theologians carefully study the works of previous practitioners. In fact, much of the impetus for their work is provided by the study of the past.

But there are also important differences. The most important one is that Christian theology is based on the assumption that certain propositions are to be accepted because they are revealed truths. In theology, that is, certain claims can be and commonly are accepted *on authority*, for example, because the Bible says so. Thus, in the pages of Christian theological works, it is quite common to find biblical references appended to arguments, references that are obviously designed to lend credence and authority to the points being made. Typical philosophers, on the other hand, require arguments, reasons, or evidence in order for some point to be acceptable. They will rarely, if ever, appeal to an authority as a reason for accepting a view. Instead, they will typically appeal to the reason or argument given for that view.

Because of this difference, some people think that philosophy and theology are enemies. Many philosophers have apparently believed this, and so have some great figures in Christian theology, from Tertullian to Karl Barth. Some even think that the apostle Paul asserted passionately that philosophy and the Christian gospel are at odds with each other: "See to it that no one takes you captive through hollow and deceptive philosophy, which depends on human tradition and the elemental spiritual forces of this world rather than on Christ" (Col. 2:8). Paul's words can easily be misinterpreted. Of course many philosophies are inimical to Christian faith, but we believe that philosophy itself—the search for answers to ultimate questions—is neutral. Some philosophers attack religion and some defend it, but philosophy itself is neither an enemy nor a friend of Christian faith.

The brief passage from Colossians should not be taken as a condemnation by Paul of all philosophy. Paul's speech at Athens recorded in Acts 17 shows how he could appreciate and even utilize the current philosophy of his day. He even appears to have quoted Stoic philosophers and poets! What Paul was criticizing were the fantastic and mythological speculations that were being perpetrated among the Colossian Christians. In effect, he was saying, "Do not allow yourselves to be deluded by empty, superstitious thought masquerading as wisdom or philosophy."

And following 1 Corinthians 1:17–25 and 2:1–14 (which you should read right now!), we agree that (1) Christian faith does not rest on philosophical wisdom but on revealed truth; (2) the truth revealed to the eyes of Christians can seem foolish to nonbelievers; (3) no rational system devised by humans, no matter how eloquently it is expressed, has the power to save souls; and (4) the true wisdom concerning God is attained not by reasoning but by faith.

But we do not hold that reasoning is divorced from faith. Although reasoning does not exhaust faith, we believe that it is a vital element in faith. Moreover, as Thomas Aquinas argued, philosophy can do some things for faith. It can help to systematically order the propositions that are accepted on faith. And it can help defend them against criticisms. Accordingly, philosophy can helpfully relate to both systematic theology and apologetics.

Not all Christians see themselves as philosophers, although, as we stated above, all Christians are philosophers to the extent that they ask ultimate questions. But some believers should try to systematize and defend the faith. Indeed, some Christians must do philosophy. For philosophically inclined persons who are also Christians, doing philosophy may be a spiritual necessity because they are incapable of believing unless their rational scruples allow it. This does not mean that the faith of such people is merely intellectual—cold, theoretical, and dispassionate. Philosophically inclined believers can be deeply and passionately committed to the faith.

WHAT IS PHILOSOPHICAL THEOLOGY?

Philosophical theology attempts to *use the methodologies and conceptual resources of philosophers and apply them to theological issues.* Now, there are certainly some theologians who approach theological issues philosophically, and we deeply admire them. But not all theologians approach theological issues armed with the assumptions, conceptual resources, or the methodologies of philosophy. Indeed, some recent and contemporary theologians have been quite resistant to philosophy and its tools.

The crucial point is that philosophical theologians, unlike those who are doing philosophy of religion, are prepared to accept the truth of crucial Christian beliefs at the outset. Some of these truths are often argued for, of course, but they are also sometimes taken as assumed premises in arguments. Philosophical theologians bring their faith commitments with them. Thus, Norman Kretzmann summarizes the discipline as follows:

> Philosophical theology shares the methods of natural theology broadly conceived—i.e., analysis and argumentation of all sorts acceptable in philosophy and the sciences—but it lifts natural theology's restrictions on premises. In particular, philosophical theology accepts as premises doctrinal propositions that are not also initially acceptable to observation and reason. From a philosophical point of view, it takes up such premises as assumptions . . . [it is] engaged in such reasoning, tests the coherence of doctrinal propositions, develops their implications, attempts explanations of them, discovers their connections with other

doctrinal propositions, and so on, with no pretense at offering proofs of the sort putatively available in natural theology.[3]

Philosophical theology, then, allows propositions concerning doctrines such as the Trinity or the incarnation to run through the rigor of philosophical scrutiny with tests of intelligibility and logical consistency. Moreover, the goal is to attain deeper understanding of Christian teaching. No sensible philosopher or theologian will deny the shroud of mystery that overhangs our thinking about God, and hence no sensible philosopher or theologian will strive for *total* comprehension or strive to remove *all* the mysteries. But the desire is to have faith seeking understanding.

What good is philosophical theology? Why is it important? When we speak of the value of philosophical theology, we are not necessarily talking about overt use of logic (syllogisms, symbols, etc.), which some philosophers use as handy tools in their own purely philosophical work. What we have in mind are the following:

(1) Avoiding obfuscation: we should write and speak clearly, so that our meaning is comprehensible (we admit that even some philosophers fail to achieve that result; nevertheless, philosophers strive for it).

(2) Making careful distinctions: we should avoid caricatures, conflation, or oversimplification of views or claims.

(3) Providing a logically consistent view: we should avoid any view that would entail a logical contradiction.

(4) Providing an intelligible view: we should be able to have some grasp of the concepts or terms being employed.

(5) Being biblically faithful: we should ensure that our views or claims do not contradict clear teaching in Scripture, and philosophical examination can help us better detect whether there are such conflicts.

---

3. Norman Kretzmann, "Reason in Mystery," in *The Philosophy in Christianity*, ed. Godfrey Vesey (Cambridge: Cambridge University Press, 1989), 15–16.

In our opinion there is far too much ignorance and intellectual sloppiness among some Christians and, unfortunately, among some church leaders. For example, in our experience we have encountered some Christians who hold to the following beliefs:

- As long as you are sincere and don't hurt anybody, God won't mind what you believe.
- The Trinity commits us to believing that 3 = 1.
- Any Christian who is suffering from disease or illness isn't praying hard enough or doesn't really trust God.
- We will live forever with God without our bodies.

Christian leaders have a responsibility to correct these sorts of errors, to instruct people as to what true Christian beliefs and practices are. We believe that philosophical theology can greatly assist in that task.

When John Wesley addressed new pastors, he expressed the importance of studying logic and philosophy in order to do theology well. In one place he wrote,

Am I a tolerable master of the sciences? Have I gone through the very gate of them, logic? If not, I am not likely to go much farther, when I stumble at the threshold. Do I understand it so as to be ever the better for it? To have it always ready for use? . . . Rather, have not my stupid indolence and laziness made me very ready to believe, what the little wits and pretty gentlemen affirm, "That logic is good for nothing?" It is good for this at least . . . to make people talk less; by showing them both what is, and what is not, to the point; and how extremely hard it is to prove anything. Do I understand metaphysics; if not the depths of the Schoolmen, the subtleties of Scotus or Aquinas, yet the first rudiments, the general principles, of that useful science?[4]

---

4. John Wesley, "An Address to the Clergy," in *The Works of the Rev. John Wesley, A.M.*, vol. 10, 4th ed. (London: John Mason, 1841), 472–73.

There is, of course, much more to doing theology than what logic and philosophy can contribute. But to us, it is not surprising that there is an array of sloppy thinking about theological matters by those who neglect to learn basic logic and philosophy.

We hope that as you go through this book, you will see what philosophical theology can contribute as we labor together in thinking and speaking about the God who has revealed himself to us.

FURTHER READINGS

Ample resources exist for studying systematic theology, apologetics, and other theological disciplines. For systematic or historical theology, you may want to consult Millard Erickson, *Christian Theology* (Grand Rapids: Baker, 1998); Wayne Grudem, *Systematic Theology* (Grand Rapids: Zondervan, 1994); or Alister McGrath, *Historical Theology* (Oxford: Wiley-Blackwell, 2013). For basic apologetics and natural theology, a good place to start is William Lane Craig, *On Guard* (Colorado Springs: David C Cook, 2010); Peter Kreeft and Ron Tacelli, *Handbook of Christian Apologetics* (Downers Grove, IL: InterVarsity Press, 1994); and Stephen T. Davis, *Rational Faith* (Downers Grove, IL: InterVarsity Press, 2016). For more advanced reading, check out William Lane Craig, *Reasonable Faith* (Wheaton, IL: Crossway, 2008).

For an introduction to philosophy, especially from a Christian perspective, we recommend J. P. Moreland and William Lane Craig, *Philosophical Foundations for a Christian Worldview*, 2nd ed. (Downers Grove, IL: InterVarsity Press, 2017). For a great introductory book on philosophy of religion, see Linda Trinkaus Zagzebski, *Philosophy of Religion: An Historical Introduction* (Malden, MA: Blackwell, 2007). For more on intellectual virtues, we recommend the website intellectualvirtues.org and the corresponding primer, *Cultivating Good Minds*, written by Jason Baehr and available for download on that site.

Not many works in philosophical theology target nonacademics, though a good place to start would be Thomas McCall, *An Invitation to Analytic Christian Theology* (Downers Grove, IL: InterVarsity Press, 2015). For more advanced and in-depth study, see Thomas Flint and Michael Rea, *Oxford Handbook of Philosophical Theology* (Oxford: Oxford University Press, 2011); and Michael Rea, *Oxford Readings in Philosophical Theology*, vols. 1 and 2 (Oxford: Oxford University Press, 2009).

REVELATION AND SCRIPTURE

If it is true, as Christians believe, that God exists and is the creator of the physical universe, including human beings, then it is natural to suppose that God would want us to know who he is and what he expects from us. That is, God would want to reveal himself to us. Christians hold that God did and does exactly that. God is not required to do so, of course. Humans have no right to receive any communication from God. That God decided to reveal himself to human creatures is a gift of grace.

What then is the purpose of divine revelation? It is to achieve God's purposes in creation. God reveals himself in order to establish a personal relationship with us, and he wants us to love, worship, and obey him. After all, apart from God's revelatory guidance, human beings might invent for themselves all sorts of false ideas and inappropriate ways of living. Our deepest spiritual problem as human beings is nicely summed up by a question that a jailer in the Asia Minor town of Philippi once asked the apostle Paul: "What must I do to be saved?" (Acts 16:30). Apart from revelation, we would have little to no idea how to answer that question; we would know very little of what we need to know.

Imagine how the question of how one can be saved might be answered without revelation. We can think of four likely answers that would have been conceived and developed by human reasoning alone:

LEGALISM: A religious system that consists only of a set of rules that must be stringently followed.

RITUALISM: A religious system that prescribes ceremonial practices, perhaps to placate the gods or to engage in a trade of goods and services—for example, sacrifices for plenty of rain and crops.

RELATIVISM: The view that no particular set of beliefs or practices is correct or privileged—as long as you are sincere in what you believe and how you live, you are doing well.

NIHILISM: There is no answer to the question or no way of knowing the answer, so there is no hope of salvation—it is merely wishful thinking.

So, if there were no divine revelation, it is likely that human beings would have come up with many false ideas pertaining to salvation. Moreover, we see these tendencies today when divinely revealed truths are neglected, especially with many who think that religion is relativistic, private, syncretistic, or deistic—or perhaps even all four!

Christians, however, believe that God has indeed revealed himself to us, and this knowledge is crucial. Some of the things we believe God has revealed to human beings are that God is triune, that Christ is divine, that Christ made atonement for humans, that we will one day be raised from the dead, and so on. We will be addressing these claims of revelation in later chapters of this book, but in this chapter we will look at the nature of divine revelation itself.

DIVINE REVELATION

A divine revelation is an unveiling or disclosing of something that was previously hidden or unknown. Most theologians distinguish between two main ways in which God has chosen to reveal himself: general revelation and special revelation. *General revelation* consists of those things about God, the world, humanity, morality, and religion that human beings can learn on their own—that is, without any supernatural ("special") assistance from God. These truths can be discovered in principle by human reason and careful reflection. The Bible appears to teach that some important truths can be learned in this way (cf. Ps. 19:1; Acts 17:22–29; Rom. 1:18–23). Theologians have suggested that we can see evidence for them, for example, in considering the beauty and grandeur of creation, in reasoning cogently about God, or maybe even in examining our own consciences. But natural revelation, even at its best, is incomplete, hazy, and easily confused.

Thomas Aquinas, a medieval theologian and philosopher, worried that even for truths about God that can be discovered by human reason alone, there are some serious concerns and limitations (*Summa Theologiae* I.1.1). For example, he claimed that if general revelation was all we had, only a few intellectuals would be able to discover these truths about God, and doing so would take a very long time and likely include many falsehoods, given human fallibility. So, natural revelation is in need of supplementation, especially since it does not tell us all that we need to know or guarantee that we will arrive at the truth.

Another reason that general revelation is insufficient is that there are huge barriers or gaps between human beings and God. Indeed, there are at least three such gaps:

(1) *Ontological gap:* God is a self-existing, eternal, and all-powerful creator, whereas we human beings are dependent, temporal, and feeble creatures.

(2) *Epistemological gap:* we are limited in our capacity to know and understand, especially to know and understand a being who is transcendent and radically different from us.

(3) *Moral gap:* God is a holy and morally perfect being, and we are depraved and self-centered creatures, and our sin separates us from God and darkens our minds to truth.

Because of these gaps, human beings naturally know little of God and his requirements, or at least not enough to comprehend God's redemptive purposes.

But thankfully God did not leave us to ourselves. We also have *special revelation*, which consists of those things about God, the world, humanity, morality, and religion that are relevant to our salvation and that we can learn only as the result of some supernatural or special act of divine assistance. Typically special revelation consists of things revealed by God to some person or group of persons through dreams, visions, epiphanies, prophecies, or miracles, though Christians believe that the ultimate way that God has specially revealed himself is through the life, teachings, death, and resurrection of Jesus Christ. Christians believe that reading the Scriptures can also, through the illumination of the Holy Spirit, speak to us and reveal God to us.

God reveals himself via special revelation in two main ways: in acts and in words. God's actions in the world include (among many others) the rescue of the children of Israel from Egyptian slavery and the resurrection of Jesus from the dead. These are miraculous deeds of God or personal encounters with God in the world. God's revelatory action of saving Israel at the Red Sea spoke volumes to Israel about the character and purposes of God. So does the resurrection of Jesus to Christians. These modes of revelation are actions; they are not verbal, at least not originally or primarily verbal.

But God also reveals himself to human beings linguistically, that is, in words. For example, the Decalogue (Ten Commandments), the oracles of the Old Testament prophets, the teachings of Jesus, and the letters of Paul all consist of words from God to human beings. And even God's revelatory actions in history are almost always accompanied by authoritative verbal interpretations. Indeed, it is not easy to see how a bare event, action, or encounter with God could be revelatory in any clear sense without interpretation or explanation. The exodus event is interpreted in Exodus 11–15; the resurrection of Jesus is explained in 1 Corinthians 15 (among other places). Interpretation is crucial because bare revelatory acts of God are easily misunderstood or forgotten over time. That can also be true of words recorded in a text, but verbal revelation is much easier to preserve and pass on. So Christians believe that God used both methods of revelation.

PHILOSOPHY AND SCRIPTURE

Suppose that God wanted to reveal himself to as many people as possible. If so, it would seem fitting for God to decide that at least part of divine revelation would be crucially located in a book. That is, God would want revelation to be potentially available to as wide a population as possible, and not just to those who were present at the time of important events, or to an elite class of scholars, or to those who were initiated into mysteries. This population would include both those who were present at the time of the original revelation but also to those who came years or even centuries later. Any book naturally first appears in a certain historical, cultural, and linguistic setting. But if the book were to be produced, distributed, and translated, it could be made available to almost anyone.

God would also have to superintend the process of the writing of the various parts of his book, ensuring that it contained, at least in large part, what God wanted it to contain. Christians typically believe that God did in fact supervise the creation, production, transmission, and preservation of the Bible. Indeed, the fact of God's providential guidance of the Bible makes it unique among all the books that have ever been written in the world's history. It reveals God in a unique and authoritative way.

Much can be said about divine revelation, general and special, both in acts and in words. However, our focus will be on the Bible—special revelation in words. That is not because the other aspects of divine revelation are not important. But given the centrality of Scripture for many Christians in the church, we think that highlighting the philosophical work in this area will be quite beneficial.

No doubt many philosophical issues arise when one thinks about Scripture. One important and ongoing debate is regarding its relation to truth. For example, Christian philosophers and theologians have argued that the Gospels (Matthew, Mark, Luke, and John) or the New Testament, or even the whole Bible, is historically reliable—that we can trust it to reveal facts about historical figures and events in the way that we can trust other reliable historical documents. A document can be reliable even if it contains some mistakes, just as a news source can be regarded as reliable even though it makes occasional reporting errors. However, many Christians want to make stronger claims about the Bible beyond asserting that it is historically reliable. For example, many maintain that the Bible is *inerrant*, meaning that it makes no errors at all—and this includes any statement in the Bible (at least in the original texts), be it on matters of faith and morals or history, science, geography, sociology, or whatever. Other philosophers and theologians hold a slightly weaker view and instead claim that the Bible is infallible. Although the term *infallibility* would come closer to meaning that something *cannot* be mistaken (and hence you would think that it is a stronger view than inerrancy, which states that the Bible *in fact* makes no error), theologians often use the term *infallibility* to mean that the Bible makes no mistakes only when it comes to matters of faith and practice—that is, with regard to what we should believe and how we should live with respect to our salvation. However, claiming that the Bible is infallible allows that the Bible might have erred about other matters, perhaps on some specific historical or empirical claim.

Another important issue some philosophers and theologians have discussed is regarding the canon of Scripture, that is, the books of the Bible. Why are some books included in the Bible and others not? Is it because of a feature that all the biblical books possess? Or is it something about the canon that confers the special status on the books? Some maintain that if a text is authoritative, it should thereby be included in the canon, whereas others argue that the fact that a text is included in the canon confers that text with its authority. We can also ask about the Bible's unity or coherence as a whole, especially since there are many different genres that appear in the Bible, such as historical narrative, moral stories, laws, poetry, wisdom literature, apocalyptic literature, epistles, and so on. Regarding the issue of reliability/inerrancy/infallibility and canon, plenty of accessible resources are available for those interested in these issues, so we will not address them here.

That said, there are two important areas in which we believe philosophical scholarship has greatly advanced the discussion concerning Scripture. The first has to do with the nature of inspiration, and the second has to do with an evaluation of historical biblical criticism, and so we will elaborate on what ways philosophical discussion has contributed to theological reflection about these issues.

INSPIRATION

The Bible was written by many different authors and editors, and their different styles of writing and uses of language are evident in the text. But Christians also believe that the Bible is the written Word of God. According to 2 Timothy 3:16, all of Scripture is "God-breathed"; that is, it is divinely inspired. There is a sense in which God is responsible for the Bible—that Scripture says what God wanted to be said. We construe divine inspiration as the influence of the Holy Spirit on the writing of the Bible. All Christians seem to agree on this much. But there remains a puzzle regarding exactly *how* the Holy Spirit inspired Scripture. How exactly can the texts of Scripture be authored by humans and by God? The Bible did not just descend down from the clouds into human hands. It was written by human beings with their own idiosyncratic styles, concerns, agendas, environments, and audiences. So there is a cultural context associated with each book of the Bible. And yet Christians affirm that God speaks to us—indeed to all Christians at all times and in all places—through the words of Scripture. So how does God accomplish this?

We will present several views regarding the nature of biblical inspiration. The accounts we examine do not exhaust all the live options with regard to biblical inspiration. We simply chose these as representative of the kind of views currently being discussed by contemporary philosophical theologians, and it would be worthwhile for readers to assess whether these accounts are plausible or whether a more satisfactory theory can be devised.

Dictation

Probably the most simplistic theory of biblical inspiration is the *dictation theory*. As the name suggests, this account maintains that God is the direct author of Scripture because God dictated to its human writers the very words they wrote down. Perhaps God did so audibly, and human authors wrote what they heard with their ears. Or perhaps the message given was transmitted directly into the minds of the authors. Whatever the case, the view functionally eliminates human agency as producing the words of Scripture; they are words from God and not from humans.

While it is not entirely clear whether any Christian actually held this view concerning biblical inspiration, some people have suggested that John Calvin appears to have accepted something like a dictation view, especially in his remark concerning the author of the gospel of Mark, claiming that it is "of little importance" knowing exactly who the author is as long "as the Holy Spirit directed him and guided his pen."[1] However, most scholars take a more nuanced interpretation to Calvin's view, arguing that Calvin would have rejected the dictation view. Once we carefully examine the views of actual theologians, virtually no Christian scholar (past or present) admits to holding such an overly simplistic view of inspiration (though some other religions do claim that their sacred texts were given through divine dictation).

Why the dictation view is such an unpopular theory should be obvious, for it does not adequately take into account the many differences in genre, style, vocabulary, and even substantive content that exists in the various books and passages of Scripture. Biblical scholarship also assumes different human authorship, analyzing texts based on the circumstances of the author, including the aim and original audience of the different books. So divine inspiration need not preclude any human influence, such as the idiosyncratic style and grammar of the authors, let alone the historical situations that may have influenced the authors'

---

1. John Calvin, "The Argument," in *Commentary a Harmony of the Evangelists, Matthew, Mark, and Luke*, vol. 1 (Grand Rapids: Christian Classics Ethereal Library), 18.

concerns. Moreover, supposing that Scripture is the product of both God and human authors is much more common, and so a theory of inspiration should adequately explain how Scripture can be produced by both.[2]

Divine Influence

The next view—which we will call the *influence theory*—avoids the model of dictation and instead strives for a view that is compatible with the biblical texts as we find them and with modern biblical scholarship.[3] God's main influence on the biblical writers, according to the influence theory, was on the ideas or concepts that the writers entertained rather than on their precise words or statements. God does speak to us in the Bible, but divine inspiration is somewhat like a teacher who inspires her students. If a teacher inspires a group of students, the students may have been inspired to different degrees, especially considering the abilities and interests of each student. Moreover, students may or may not agree with their teacher, but the mark of a teacher's influence may pervade what the student does or says as long as the student's view or method does not widely diverge from the teacher's view. Accordingly, students can make mistakes while still being inspired and influenced by their teacher. The same goes for divine inspiration, according to the influence view. God's influence is pervasive and reflected in the Bible by its influence over the concepts and ideas espoused by the authors, and hence it can be truly said that it is a book inspired by God.

Although this view ends up with a Bible that is authoritative for Christian faith and practice, some worry that the influence view is not a robust enough account of inspiration. After all, even though a student may be influenced by her teacher, when the student later writes a paper, it would be a little strange to say that the teacher is the author of the paper. Similarly, even if the biblical authors were influenced by God, the divine influence theory has difficulty in maintaining that God

---

2. This is not to deny that there may be some passages in Scripture—perhaps some prophetic words—that were perhaps given by dictation or something much like it.

3. William Abraham, *The Divine Inspiration of Holy Scripture* (Oxford: Oxford University Press, 1981).

is in some substantive sense the author of the Bible. Hence, there is a concern that the divine influence theory goes too far in the opposite direction of the dictation theory—that it does not provide an adequate conception of God as author of Scripture.

Another objection to the influence theory is that such a view allows for divine inspiration outside of Scripture, including works that followed after the texts of the Bible were written. For example, it is likely that Aristotle was a student of Plato and was greatly influenced by him, and yet other philosophers can be equally if not more so impacted and influenced by the life and ideas of Plato. So if biblical inspiration consists in the inspiration of ideas, then some postbiblical prophets may be able to claim to have been inspired or divinely influenced in a similar way. If so, it is unclear why the Bible should be regarded as a uniquely inspired or uniquely authoritative text, especially if postbiblical authors or works can be influenced to the same or a greater degree.

Proponents of the influence theory may respond to this objection by claiming that authority is attached to what has been specially revealed and not merely to texts or messages that have been divinely inspired. But perhaps some who claim to be inspired (in the sense of the influence theory) can also claim to have discovered specially revealed truths (that is, truths not accessible by human reason alone), and so it seems that such messages would be regarded as authoritative as Scripture. But Scripture is typically regarded as having a unique mark of authority, so even attaching authority to special revelation and not to divine inspiration fails to capture adequately the unique authority of Scripture.

Divine Discourse

Let us next consider what we will call the *appropriated discourse view*, which points out that occasionally a piece of speech or writing can be correctly attributed to a certain person although it was originally composed by someone else.[4] For example, a secretary who knows the

---

4. Nicholas Wolterstorff, *Divine Discourse* (Cambridge: Cambridge University Press, 1995).

mind of the boss is asked by the boss to compose a letter. After reading it, the boss approves of the letter and signs it, whereby it becomes the boss's letter. Another example is when ambassadors are entitled to "speak in the name" of the head of state whom they represent; they may have written something down and addressed others with the content, but the content can be regarded as coming from the state leader.

Naturally, there can be different modes and degrees of superintendence over the words and different degrees in which the final words of the text are authorized and accepted as one's own by the person who counts as the author. We even see in the Bible examples of (non-divine) appropriated discourse. Some scholars suggest that the books of Romans and 1 Corinthians (and others) were written by scribes, but those words were appropriated by Paul, which is why he may have indicated that he was writing with his own hand (Rom. 16:22; 1 Cor. 16:21). So appropriated discourse is not an unfamiliar practice in either history or contemporary times.

The claim that the Bible is divinely inspired, and so is in a sense God's book, can be understood as divinely appropriated human discourse. Accordingly, in the Bible God speaks to us via words that were composed by other people, namely, the Bible's human authors. But through appropriated discourse, God is to be regarded as the author of Scripture since it contains content "approved and signed" by God (so to speak).

While an interesting approach, the appropriated discourse view does not provide a complete theory of divine inspiration. In fact, some proponents of this view recognize that the notion of appropriated discourse needs to be supplemented. Many theologians have a hard time believing that God had nothing whatsoever to do with the composition of the books of the Bible—as though God saw the books lying around and simply decided to adopt the words as his own. Nevertheless, this view allows a way for human discourse to mediate God's speaking to us.

The last two views of inspiration discussed do not mention a way in which God could ensure attaining the exact words he wanted to convey to humans. No doubt there are some who think that such an approach would demand too much involvement by God, which is why they balk at adding more to divine influence or appropriated discourse. However, many Christian thinkers have held a view that is often known as *verbal plenary inspiration*; that is, all of the words of Scripture have been inspired. Without appealing to dictation, which would be an unattractive theory of verbal plenary inspiration, how can God guarantee that we have the exact words God intended to be stated in Scripture? We'll finish our discussion of inspiration by examining two proposals.

Theological Determinism

One way of ensuring that the Bible contains all the words God intended would be by appealing to *theological determinism*, which is the view that every event has been guaranteed to have been given some aspect or attribute of God, either his will or his foreknowledge. Theological determinism enables us to quickly solve the puzzle of how Scripture can be both the words of God and the words of human beings. The answer is that God determined that the human authors wrote down exactly what he wanted them to write, and so Scripture is a product of both humans and God. Usually those who make this sort of claim endorse a view known as *compatibilism*, which claims that humans can be free and responsible even though their actions have been determined by God. So, the human authors freely wrote down what they did, but God guaranteed that the words of Scripture are as he intended them to be because he determined that the human authors acted according to his divine will.

There are some concerns over this approach. The first, of course, comes from those who reject theological determinism. Some reject it for purely philosophical reasons, usually offering arguments for incompatibilism, which claims that human freedom and responsibility are incompatible with determinism. Given incompatibilism, if the human authors wrote their parts of the Bible down freely, then their actions cannot have been determined by God; and if God determined their actions, then they cannot have acted freely.

Another concern raised against theological determinism is in the difficulty of squaring the view with the so-called problem of evil. That is, if God could determine human actions such that he could guarantee that people act exactly as he wants while retaining human freedom, then how could there be any evil in this world since God could guarantee that all human beings choose what is good? Moreover, if God could ensure that everyone would freely choose him, then why do some people end up in hell? Because of this last problem, some argue that theological determinism implies universalism, that everyone will eventually make it to heaven—and we will discuss more on hell and universalism in chapter 7. Given these considerations, some philosophers argue that an incompatibilist view of human freedom allows for a more promising way of responding to the problem of evil (though this claim is quite contentious!).

Considerations of free will aside, there is another reason why we think appealing to theological determinism is not a satisfactory theory, or at least why it provides an incomplete answer to divine inspiration even if one accepts theological determinism. For, if theological determinism is true, then God not only determined the words of Scripture but also the words of *The Odyssey* and *The Divine Comedy*, for God determined that Homer (or whoever the author was) and Dante would write exactly what they did—especially if one believes that God determined every action and event in the world. But clearly the latter two works, great as they are, are not inspired in the same sense that Scripture is said to be inspired. So merely determining what the biblical authors wrote does not by itself provide an adequate theory of inspiration, even if it ensures that they wrote exactly what God wanted—for that would be true for every author and every book, especially if God determines every human action. So theological determinism requires significant supplement if it is to work as a viable theory of divine inspiration.

Middle Knowledge

One final approach that we will consider (though there are others) is based on the notion of *middle knowledge*, a complex and somewhat controversial notion developed by the Jesuit philosopher Luis de Molina (1535–1600). According to Molina, God's knowledge can be categorized into three types: natural knowledge, middle knowledge, and free knowledge. God's natural knowledge includes his knowledge of all necessities and possibilities, that is, of what *could* be (e.g., "possibly Jacob married Rachel first and then Leah") or what *must* be (e.g., "necessarily, triangles have three sides"). God's free knowledge includes his knowledge of all true propositions that are not necessary (e.g., "Barack Obama is president of the United States from 2009 to 2017"). These propositions are usually called *contingently true propositions*—propositions that are true but could have been false. But another type of knowledge, according to Molina, is God's middle knowledge: God's knowledge of what *would* be the case if certain nonactual states of affairs obtained (e.g., "If Stephen Davis were offered a peanut butter cookie as a bribe to vote for some candidate whom he opposes, then he would refuse"). So through his middle knowledge, God can know what any person or even possible person would freely decide to do in any situation in which that person might be placed. These propositions are in the *subjunctive* mood and hence are often called *subjunctive conditionals* or *counterfactuals* (since the antecedent of the conditions are often contrary to actual fact). God's knowledge of these subjunctives or counterfactuals is called *middle knowledge* because it is logically situated between God's natural knowledge and free knowledge. But God has all his knowledge at once and eternally. So this view does not say that first God has natural knowledge, then middle knowledge, and then free knowledge. God has all of his knowledge at the same time. But, according to Molina, there is a logical ordering to God's knowledge.

Note that through his middle knowledge, God can providentially govern people without taking away their free will, thereby bringing about the results he desires. And this can be accomplished without appealing to theological determinism, for what God knows is what someone would freely do (in the incompatibilist sense of human freedom) in any particular circumstance.

Some philosophers have used the notion of middle knowledge to make sense of God's providence as well as to explain how God's foreknowledge and human freedom can be made consistent. But in the context of our discussion, the notion of middle knowledge has been used to develop an account of verbal plenary inspiration while maintaining that the Bible is authored by both God and human beings.

The way that middle knowledge can be employed in a theory of inspiration is by the fact that God can know what someone would write if placed in a certain circumstance.[5] So God knows what the apostle Paul would write in a certain circumstance at a certain time, and so God actualizes only those circumstances where human beings freely write down what God desires to be written down. Thus, the scriptural texts are truly the work of its human authors, who wrote what they did freely. But they are also truly the work of God since God superintended the very words of Scripture by bringing about those very circumstances that would result in the words God desired to be included in Scripture. And unlike the previous theory that involved theological determinism, there is a way to distinguish between Scripture and other texts, for it may be that the words of Scripture are what God wanted to be written down, whereas the words of *The Odyssey* might not have been what God wanted (but were brought about by Homer insofar as God created Homer and placed him in a particular circumstance). So this appears to be at least one advantage of the middle knowledge approach over the theological deterministic view.

The concept of middle knowledge clearly has some utility in making sense of several important theological doctrines (providence, foreknowledge, divine inspiration). However, some philosophers have argued that there is no such thing as middle knowledge, insisting that God has only natural knowledge and free knowledge. Another problem for proponents of middle knowledge arises when we try to understand what makes the propositions of middle knowledge true. Consider

---

5. William Lane Craig, "Men Moved by the Holy Spirit Spoke from God: A Middle Knowledge Perspective on Biblical Inspiration," *Philosophia Christi* 1 (1999): 45–82.

the statement "If Peter were in an ice cream store, he would choose bubblegum-flavored ice cream." This is something God was supposed to know before God created the world. But what makes that statement true before the creation of the world? Some have argued that there isn't anything to make it true. So there doesn't seem to be plausible grounds for the propositions of middle knowledge; but true propositions cannot be groundless. Therefore, some philosophers have abandoned the very idea of middle knowledge.

Other philosophers have claimed that God does not have counterfactual knowledge but rather knows a weaker proposition of what humans would *probably* do in any particular circumstance, especially if incompatibilism about free will is true. That is, God doesn't know this proposition: "If Peter were in an ice cream store, he would choose bubblegum-flavored ice cream." After all, if one rejects theological determinism and claims that one freely chooses from a range of options, it may be difficult to know exactly what someone would do. Instead, some argue that what God knows instead is this proposition: "If Peter were in an ice cream store, he would *probably* choose bubblegum-flavored ice cream." The debate over middle knowledge, then, is quite complex but worth exploring.

Aside from the views canvassed here, there are several other views and issues concerning inspiration. For example, some claim that there are different levels of inspiration. Others suggest that God did not inspire individual writers but groups of people, perhaps specific communities that were instrumental in bringing about and editing certain biblical texts.

We invite readers to think about each of these views of divine inspiration of Scripture and consider which view is the most plausible. Or perhaps another account of divine inspiration should be defended, one that avoids some of the concerns that have been raised against the accounts discussed so far. It may even be the case that no single theory of biblical inspiration covers the entire biblical canon. Perhaps different theories will be relevant to different texts. For example, we might think that the Ten Commandments were dictated, whereas other passages were inspired either through appropriated discourse or by way of middle knowledge. So a complex theory of biblical inspiration, one that combines several approaches, is another live option.

HISTORICAL BIBLICAL CRITICISM

As most students of the Bible are aware, interpreting Scripture is no easy task and requires serious and careful study. It seems fair to say that most Christians studying Scripture would regard it as authoritative and trustworthy, especially since it has been divinely inspired (in some sense or other), and hence we can believe many of the central tenets of Christianity that we learn from reading Scripture.

Over the last two hundred years, a practice we call *historical biblical criticism* (sometimes also called *higher criticism* or *historical critical scholarship*) has gained traction among many serious biblical scholars. Historical biblical criticism is not one methodology but more of a family of approaches to studying Scripture, but one of its main features is to understand and interpret the books of Scripture utilizing only the empirical methods of history and science. That is, the way to interpret the Bible is to study it in the way we would approach any other historical document. Accordingly, scholars need to be relying on other historical documents, archaeological discoveries, the results of scientific data, and so forth. Much of the focus rests on discovering how the texts were composed and from what source or sources they are derived. In fact, some proponents and practitioners of historical biblical criticism suggest that this approach is the only (scientifically) respectable way to study and interpret the Bible.

To be sure, we do not repudiate historical biblical criticism but in fact regard it as a useful tool in one's overall study of the Bible. However, some proponents of historical biblical criticism have ended up with conclusions that are opposed to traditional Christian beliefs.

These theological revisionists end up reaching conclusions that are inimical to traditional Christian faith, usually in the denial of miraculous occurrences (such as the resurrection) or the divinity of Christ.[6] In fact, one proponent of historical biblical criticism makes it sound as though Jesus's teachings affirm that there is no God—that is, that Jesus's message affirms atheism![7]

Christian philosophers, however, have examined some of these approaches and their assumptions, and many of them conclude that these challenges to traditional Christian beliefs are themselves problematic and so do not threaten the Christian faith. One thing philosophers are proficient at is exposing some of the unquestioned assumptions of an approach or methodology. One assumption that is held by some practitioners of historical biblical criticism is the claim that natural laws hold in such a way that divine intervention is impossible, thereby concluding that God could not directly act in the world—and therefore miracles could never happen, and so all the miracle stories of the Bible are to be understood solely as mythology or fictional narrative and not as historical report. But some philosophers have recognized that such an assumption need not be accepted by Christians, especially if they believe and have good reasons to believe that God exists and acts in the world.[8] If an argument were given for the impossibility of divine intervention, Christians would have to address it. But usually no argument is provided by proponents of historical biblical criticism—it is often just assumed by its practitioners. So then why should Christians, or anyone for that matter, accept it?

There are also weaker approaches to historical biblical criticism.[9] Instead of claiming that divine intervention is impossible,

6. For example, see Ernst Troeltsch, "Historiography," in *Encyclopedia of Religion and Ethics*, ed. J. Hastings (New York: Scribner, 1967).

7. Thomas Sheehan, *The First Coming* (New York: Random House, 1986).

8. See Alvin Plantinga, *Knowledge and Christian Belief* (Grand Rapids: Eerdmans, 2015), chap. 8. For more in-depth discussion on historical biblical criticism, see Plantinga, *Where the Conflict Really Lies: Science, Religion, and Naturalism* (Oxford: Oxford University Press, 2011), chaps. 5–6.

9. For example, see John Meier, *A Marginal Jew: Rethinking the Historical Jesus*, vols. 1–2 (New York: Doubleday, 1991).

some practitioners of historical biblical criticism simply try to interpret Scripture without any theological or substantive philosophical assumption—that is, they try to be as neutral as possible as they inquire into the historicity and veracity of the biblical texts. Here is how philosopher Alvin Plantinga summarizes their stance:

> You do not invoke or employ any theological assumptions or presuppositions. You do not assume . . . that the Bible is inspired by God in any special way, or contains anything like specifically divine discourse. You do not assume that Jesus is the divine Son of God, or that he arose from the dead, or that his suffering and death is in some way a propitiatory atonement for human sin. . . . You do not assume any of these things because in pursuing science, one does not assume or employ any proposition which one knows by faith.[10]

We do think this kind of study can indeed be beneficial insofar as it has much to teach us about the way in which many of the biblical documents have been composed, collected, edited, or organized. However, even this weaker approach may lead to claims that conflict with traditional Christian belief, because such an approach may yield the conclusion that Christ was not raised from the dead.

Again, Christian philosophers have pointed out that even if this latter exercise in biblical interpretation is worthwhile, Christians need not limit themselves only to the deliverances of historical biblical criticism. They can also rely on arguments for God's existence, the reliability of New Testament documents, the historicity of Jesus's life, death, and resurrection, and so on. Moreover, readers of the Bible can also rely on their own experiences or the inward testimony of the Holy Spirit. To use only the resources of historical biblical criticism and to neglect these other sources of knowledge severely restricts what can be known from scriptural texts.

---

10. Alvin Plantinga, "Two (or More) Kinds of Scripture Scholarship," *Modern Theology* 14 (1998): 251.

As an analogy, it would be similar to someone closing her eyes and trying to discover what is in a room by deciding not to move and not to touch anything but using only her sense of smell and hearing. She might be able to detect several things about the room—perhaps she will detect a clock if she hears ticking, or perhaps she will detect some coffee if she smells it brewing. But there will be so much more that she is unable to detect without utilizing her vision, her sense of touch, and her ability to move about the room. Similarly, practitioners of historical biblical criticism require that we limit our resources and then demand that we accept only the findings from such limitations. But other resources are available for Christians to use, and these additional sources may provide us with information that supports traditional Christian beliefs (such as God's existence or Christ's resurrection).

In these discussions, it has become clear that a more general epistemological point is being made. Many proponents of historical biblical criticism suggest that there is only one acceptable method (or set of methods) of inquiry that is legitimate when studying Scripture. But the critics of historical biblical criticism have argued that "if we employ all that we know (not just natural empirical reason), we stand a much better chance of getting close to the actual full-orbed truth."[11] The general epistemological claim, then, is this: it is better to use all of the relevant resources available to us when appropriate in acquiring knowledge than to restrict the resources one can employ. If this is correct, then historical biblical criticism needs to retool its epistemological framework.

Philosophers throughout history have examined intellectual pursuits and methodologies, explicating the limits as well as the virtues and vices of such approaches. In just this way, some philosophers have recognized the limits, virtues, and vices of historical biblical criticism. Much can be gleaned from historical biblical criticism—and so it does not need to be rejected wholesale—but its undefended assumptions can be exposed as

---

11. Alvin Plantinga, "Sheehan's Shenanigans: How Theology Becomes Tomfoolery," in *The Analytic Theist: An Alvin Plantinga Reader,* ed. James Sennett (Grand Rapids: Eerdmans, 1998), 327.

well as its limitations in exactly what it can deliver. Philosophers, then, have plenty to learn from historians and biblical scholars, but they also have much to contribute to the historical study of Scripture.

CONCLUDING THOUGHTS

A deep connection exists between the inspiration of the Bible, as traditionally conceived, and the authority of the Bible. This connection seems sensible: if a book has been so guided throughout the history of its production that God speaks to us in it and fulfills God's redemptive purposes for it, then that book will naturally have a great deal of authority. Our beliefs and behavior as human beings ought to be guided by it.

But you might be wondering what this means concretely for readers of the Bible. We think it means, among other things, that Christians have a certain attitude toward the Bible. That is, we believe what it says, we trust it, we lay ourselves open to it, and we allow our beliefs to be influenced by it. We accept the truth of the assertions that we find in it. It also means taking the questions that we find in the Bible (e.g., Romans 6:1: "Shall we go on sinning so that grace may increase?") as legitimate and probing questions. Further, it means taking biblical exhortations (e.g., Psalm 136:1: "Give thanks to the LORD, for he is good") as exhortations addressed to us so that we must take heed. And it also means taking poetic sections of the Bible (e.g., Psalm 100:3: "We are his people, the sheep of his pasture") as powerful and affective expressions of the way reality is.

In short, we trust the Bible to guide our lives. We allow our lives to be influenced by it. We intend to listen when it speaks. We consider it normative. We look to it for comfort, encouragement, challenge, warning, guidance, and instruction. You might say that we submit to the Bible. We place ourselves under its theological and moral authority. We approach the Bible with a hermeneutic of trust. We take it as the source of religious truth above all other sources, the norm or guide to religious truth above all other norms or guides.

All of this depends on our view that the Bible is a special book, a book unlike all other books, a book through which in some strong sense *God speaks to us*. As we have seen, Christians may not agree on how to interpret that last claim. And we have seen that it takes serious study and effort, requiring the employment of various approaches and methods. However, we maintain that Christians should at least agree on this: that the Bible is and ought to be the central way in which God exercises authority over the lives of individual believers and over the life of the Christian church.

FURTHER READINGS

For an advanced treatment of some of these themes, see Stephen T. Davis, "Revelation and Inspiration," in Thomas Flint and Michael Rea, eds., *Oxford Handbook of Philosophical Theology* (Oxford: Oxford University Press, 2011); and Richard Swinburne, *Revelation* (Oxford: Oxford University Press, 2007). For some substantive arguments in the debate over inerrancy versus infallibility, see Stephen T. Davis, *The Debate about the Bible: Inerrancy vs. Infallibility* (Louisville, KY: Westminster John Knox, 1977). On the influence theory of biblical inspiration, see William Abraham, *The Divine Inspiration of Holy Scripture* (Oxford: Oxford University Press, 1981). For more on appropriated discourse, see Nicholas Wolterstorff, *Divine Discourse* (Cambridge: Cambridge University Press, 1995). And for the Molinist view on inspiration, see William Lane Craig, "Men Moved by the Holy Spirit Spoke from God: A Middle Knowledge Perspective on Biblical Inspiration," *Philosophia Christi* 1 (1999): 45–82. For serious evaluation of historical biblical criticism, see Alvin Plantinga, "Two (or More) Kinds of Scripture Scholarship," *Modern Theology* 14 (1998): 243–78, and Eleonore Stump, "Visits to the Sepulcher and Biblical Exegesis," *Faith and Philosophy* 6 (1989): 353–77.

THE TRIUNE GOD

The doctrine of the Trinity clearly distinguishes Christianity from other monotheistic religions such as Judaism and Islam. Although the Trinity has played a crucial role in the theology and worship of the church throughout its history, we have noticed some patterns of neglect on this doctrine in sermons and study materials. One possible reason is that the doctrine of the Trinity might appear irrelevant to the life and practice of the ordinary Christian. But church history and recent theological scholarship demonstrate just how crucial the doctrine is to our relationship with God and our worship of him. For example, C. S. Lewis included belief in the Trinity as part of the essential core of "mere Christianity" and highlighted the Trinitarian structure of our worship and prayer.[1]

Another reason that the doctrine of the Trinity may be ignored or avoided is that it appears extremely confusing or perhaps flat-out incomprehensible. There is one God, and yet there are three persons who are God—so it looks as though there are actually three Gods. Taken superficially, the doctrine looks to be saying something that is impossible. This confusion has occasionally led some Christians into saying that concerning God we should accept the equation that three equals one ($3 = 1$). Such a pronouncement makes it seem as though Christians are required to give up on reasoning or rationality—or that Christians are really bad at math! In church we often hear that Jesus

---

1. C. S. Lewis, *Mere Christianity* (repr., New York: HarperOne, 2017), book 4, ch. 2.

Christ is God, and other times that he is the Son of God. And these two claims are often made in the same sermon without further explanation. But how can someone be the son of himself?

In this chapter we seek to help elucidate the doctrine by explicitly stating what the Christian commitments are in accepting the doctrine of the Trinity. We then present several recent proposals that try to make sense of the doctrine. These different approaches are currently being debated by many theologians and philosophers, which shows that there is no single way that Christians construe the doctrine of the Trinity. We hope that readers will be convinced that the doctrine is not contradictory but is in fact logically coherent. However, offering a logically coherent account of the doctrine of the Trinity is not an intellectually simplistic endeavor. Usually those who offer simple answers do not realize that they may be making serious logical, philosophical, or theological errors.

We leave it to you to reflect on this doctrine and decide which account of the Trinity you take to be the most plausible as you read Scripture and continue to study this profound and central teaching. We do not expect that all questions concerning the Trinity will be answered. The doctrine is a mystery and will remain mysterious to us in this life. But we desire for Christians to think more clearly and consistently about the Trinity and, by doing so, to avoid making egregious errors that not only may be contrary to God's revelation but may also be leading us astray from the way God wants us to worship and relate to him.

REASONS FOR BELIEVING IN THE TRINITY

So why do Christians accept the doctrine of the Trinity? Most Christians accept it as a truth that has been specially revealed to us by God through Scripture or through conciliar pronouncements such as the ecumenical creeds. However, a few Christians in history and even now have offered philosophical arguments in an attempt to show that the Godhead must contain within itself more than one person. The most notable historical theologian to have done so is Richard of Saint Victor (c. 1110–73). Adapting some of his ideas, contemporary philosophical theologians have offered their own arguments. Before looking at the scriptural and creedal data, we will present one of the recent philosophical arguments for a Trinitarian God.

The argument starts with the fact that God is perfect and is perfect in love (1 John 4:8). Loving another person is a great good, and if God were to miss out on such a high and wonderful thing, then it seems that there would be a significant deficiency in God. But since God is perfect, God must experience loving another person. But God is a self-existing, self-sufficient being who did not have to create the world—and so it is possible that God is the only being who exists. But if it is possible for God alone to exist and yet God must love another person, then there must be more than one person in God who love each other. Therefore, there must be more than one person in God. Notice that this argument does not lead to the conclusion that in God there are exactly three persons. But it does give us reason for rejecting that in God there can be only one person, and so this argument would rule out the unitarian view that God is a single person.[2]

Some philosophical theologians have gone even further, arguing that there must be *exactly* three persons in God. After accepting the previous argument, someone might suppose that there is still something missing in a perfectly loving being. When two people love each other, their love is directed toward one another. But often lovers desire sharing in some activity in which they can direct their love onto someone or something besides the two of them. As an example, two romantic partners may seek to have a child or to adopt a puppy, and their love for each other is enhanced insofar as they can share in loving someone else. Similarly, two divine persons who love one another would be missing out on another high and wonderful thing if they were not sharing in

---

2. For a more elaborate version of this argument, see Stephen T. Davis, "Perichoretic Monotheism," in *Christian Philosophical Theology* (Oxford: Oxford University Press, 2006).

loving someone else. And hence there must be three divine persons who each love one another and who share and cooperate with another person in loving a third.[3]

A natural question arises: Why not a fourth divine person? But as the argument goes, no void would be filled in having a fourth person. Three persons is the minimal number required to have mutual love between two persons and to share in loving someone else. Since having three divine persons is enough to experience perfect love, then there is no need to have a fourth, fifth, or any higher number of divine persons. So, in God there are three and only three divine persons.

Unsurprisingly, some philosophical theologians have criticized these arguments.[4] Does perfect love really require loving another person? Would God be missing out if a single divine person only loved himself? Some critics argue that God appears to be missing out on many high and wonderful things—for example, being a biological parent or being a sibling—and yet no one suggests that God is any less perfect by not undertaking these activities. This should lead Christians to think harder about what is required for perfect love.

Whether or not these arguments are successful, most Christians have accepted the doctrine of the Trinity on the basis of special revelation, and many claim that a traditional view of the Trinity provides the best framework for making sense of the data given to us in Scripture.[5] Scripture affirms that there is one and only one God; Christianity is, after all, a monotheistic religion. The Old Testament Shema, the declaration that the Lord our God is one (Deut. 6:4), was reaffirmed by Christ (Mark 12:29) and therefore is nonnegotiable for Christians.

---

3. This argument is adapted from Richard Swinburne, *The Christian God* (Oxford: Oxford University Press, 1994).

4. See, for example, Dale Tuggy, "On the Possibility of a Single Perfect Person," in *Christian Philosophy of Religion*, ed. Colin Ruloff (Notre Dame, IN: University of Notre Dame Press, 2015).

5. Some Christians have argued that the doctrine of the Trinity can be deduced from certain claims from Scripture, though we think that a more plausible case will employ abductive reasoning—that the traditional doctrine of the Trinity best explains all the relevant data provided in Scripture.

Moreover, Christians also believe that God the Father, Jesus Christ, and the Holy Spirit are introduced in Scripture with some indication that all three persons are divine. We won't be going into the relevant details of this last claim, but all three persons are regarded in Scripture and the creeds as being worthy of worship. Christ is depicted as having received worship by humans (Matt. 28:9) and angels (Heb. 1:6). And the Holy Spirit is invoked in the blessing of 2 Corinthians 13:14, which suggests that he, too, is worthy of worship. But we can worship only God. So Christians have traditionally affirmed that the Father, the Son, and the Holy Spirit are each God.

Christians also believe that God the Father, God the Son, and God the Spirit are distinct persons. When Jesus was being baptized, someone else was saying, "This is my Son, whom I love; with him I am well pleased" (Matt. 3:17). This was not an occasion where Jesus was talking to himself (and the Holy Spirit appeared to be present in the form of a dove). And Jesus told his disciples that although he would leave and not be bodily present with them, he would send a helper and a comforter, the Holy Spirit (John 14:26; 16:7). But Jesus wasn't saying that he would send himself, nor was he saying that the Father would be sent. So the Father, the Son, and the Spirit are regarded as three distinct persons.

These claims are also affirmed in the Christian tradition, especially in the creeds and conciliar pronouncements in church history. For example, the Niceno-Constantinopolitan creed (which many refer to as "the Nicene Creed"), formulated at the Council of Constantinople in 380–81, states that Jesus Christ is *consubstantial* with the Father— that is, Jesus Christ and the Father are of the same substance or same essence. Since the substance or essence of the Father is divine, Jesus Christ is also divine. The same creed states that the Holy Spirit is worshiped along with the Father and the Son, which appears to indicate the Holy Spirit's divine status.

These claims are even more explicitly stated in the Athanasian Creed. Here are some excerpts that highlight some of the main Trinitarian claims:

> For the person of the Father is a distinct person, the person of the Son is another, and that of the Holy Spirit still another. But the divinity of the Father, Son, and Holy Spirit is one. . . . Thus the Father is God, the Son is God, the Holy Spirit is God. Yet there are not three gods; there is but one God. Thus the Father is Lord, the Son is Lord, the Holy Spirit is Lord. Yet there are not three lords; there is but one Lord.

So we get explicit affirmation that there are three distinct persons, each of whom is God. And yet the creed strongly affirms the monotheistic claim that there is one God.

Some Christians think that although the Trinity is a mystery, there is no paradox or contradiction since what is affirmed is that there are *three persons* and *one God*. The official formulation of the fourth century is that in God there are three *hypostases* (individual substances) and one *ousia* (nature or essence).[6] So Christians are not claiming that "three equals one." There would be an obvious contradiction if Christians claimed that there are three Gods and one God, or if they said that there are three divine persons and one divine person. Rather, Christians claim that there are three different "somethings" and one "something else," and there is no obvious impossibility with that. For example, there is no contradiction in saying that there are three dogs and one pound, just as there is no contradiction in saying that there are three human beings—father, mother, and child—and one family. However, we are not out of the woods yet. For given what Christians affirm in the previous paragraphs, there may still be the concern of logical incoherence lurking, which we will discuss in depth in the next section.

We won't be discussing the historical development of the doctrine, especially as based on Scripture and the early creeds, for an abundance

---

6. The historical development of this doctrine during this period is much more complicated than suggested here. For some explanation of the nuances, we suggest reading some of the chapters in the section "Patristic Witness" in *The Trinity*, ed. Stephen T. Davis, Daniel Kendall, SJ, and Gerald O'Collins, SJ (Oxford: Oxford University Press, 1999).

of books that present such material are already available. But we invite readers to study and reflect on biblical passages such as Matthew 11:27; Mark 12:29; John 1:1–14; 14:16–17; 17:5–26; Acts 5:3–4; Romans 3:29–30; Colossians 1:15–20; and Hebrews 1:8–12, just to choose a few.

THE LOGICAL PROBLEM

From what we discussed so far, traditional Christianity requires believing at least three claims about the Trinity:

(1) The Father is God, the Son is God, and the Holy Spirit is God.
(2) The Father is not the Son, the Son is not the Holy Spirit, and the Father is not the Holy Spirit.
(3) There is one and only one God.

Even if we say that there are three persons and one God, claims (1)–(3) may still involve a contradiction. Addressing this issue is usually called the *logical problem of the Trinity* by philosophers and the *threeness-oneness problem* by theologians. Of course, thinking hard about the doctrine of the Trinity involves much more than solving the logical problem of the Trinity, but Christians should be able to articulate the doctrine while avoiding contradiction, especially since giving up any of (1)–(3) does not appear to be an option for traditional Christian belief.

From (1)–(3), let us consider two interpretations in which the threat of contradiction is looming. The interpretations depend on how we understand the meaning of "is" employed in these sentences. One way is to interpret it as the *is of identity*, and the other is to interpret it as the *is of predication*.

Suppose we interpret the statement in (1) as using the is of identity. If so, then when we say "the Father is God," we are thinking of that statement along the lines of claims such as "Clark Kent is Superman" (or Clark Kent = Superman). Under this interpretation, what we mean is that the Father is identical to God—they are one and the same thing. The same would go for "the Son is God," that the Son and God are identical. We all learned in math class that if a is identical to b, and b is identical to c, then a is identical to c, which is the property of transitivity. So interpreting (1) along these lines, we get

Father = God,
Son = God.

And by the symmetry of identity (that is, if $a = b$, then $b = a$), the last claim is equivalent to

God = Son.

And by the transitivity of identity, we can derive

Father = Son.

But claim (2) states that the Father is *not* the Son, which is naturally understood as saying that the Father and the Son are numerically distinct persons. Hence, (2) includes the claim that

Father ≠ Son.

So this simplistic and perhaps even straightforward way of interpreting (1) and (2) by using the "is of identity" leads to a clear contradiction.

Perhaps "the Father is God" doesn't make an identity claim like the statement about Clark Kent and Superman. Perhaps it should be understood as employing the "is of predication," such as the claim "Elijah is smart." That claim does not say that Elijah is identical to smartness—there are many other smart people (plus, smartness is a quality, and Elijah is not a quality; he has qualities). But even if that is how we interpret the Trinitarian claims, (1)–(3) may still be logically inconsistent, which means that not all three can be true. To make the tension clearer, suppose we assert that Rover is a dog, Fluffy is a dog, and Spot is a dog, and suppose we also say that Rover, Fluffy, and Spot are all distinct from each other. It looks like we are forced to conclude that there are three dogs. Similarly, suppose that we claim with (1) and (2) that the Father is God, the Son is God, and the Holy Spirit is God, and that the three divine persons are distinct. We then seem forced to claim that there are three Gods, and so the acceptance of (1) and (2) requires rejecting (3). Therefore, accepting all three claims would require accepting a contradiction.[7]

Even if Christians will never have a full understanding of the Trinity, we should say enough to avoid a contradiction. Throughout church history, Christian theologians have thought this could be accomplished, while humbly acknowledging that the Trinitarian doctrine will never be totally comprehensible to us, at least in this life.

Broadly speaking, there have been two main approaches that can be traced to two different Christian traditions. The first approach is often labeled *social Trinitarianism* and is considered to have been influenced by Eastern, Greek-speaking theologians from the fourth century AD, in particular the so-called Cappadocian fathers: Gregory of Nyssa, Gregory of Nazianzus, and Basil of Caesarea. The other approach is often labeled *Latin Trinitarianism* and is thought to have been influenced by Western, Latin-speaking theologians throughout the medieval period, most notably Augustine and Thomas Aquinas. Much has been written on the history of these theological traditions, some of which elaborates on this rough characterization and some that questions or challenges the characterization itself. For example, some theologians

---

7. To be clear, we are not suggesting that one cannot interpret some of these claims while using the *is of identity* or the *is of predication* (and many social Trinitarians make use of the latter notion of "is"). We are only trying to show that these straightforward interpretations lead to contradiction, and hence Christians must say more about how they understand (1)–(3) in order to avoid logical incoherence.

think that there really weren't two different approaches; they instead suggest that both Greek and Latin theologians were pretty much saying the same thing with slightly different points of emphasis.[8]

Regardless of the historical scholarship, many theories by contemporary philosophers and theologians can be grouped as either a social Trinitarian view or a Latin Trinitarian view. There are also some recent views that do not fit into either category, and some that require deviating from standard ways of understanding concepts like identity. Regarding the two main approaches, one way of distinguishing them is to think of social Trinitarianism as starting with three divine persons or centers of consciousness, where a person or a center of consciousness is similar to how we would understand these concepts in contemporary psychology. With this starting point, social Trinitarianism needs to explain the oneness of God. Latin Trinitarianism, on the other hand, usually begins by focusing on a single self and then trying to explain how there can be "threeness" in God.

Whatever view one adopts, there are some pitfalls to avoid, all of which have been deemed as heresies in church history. First, we need to avoid the heresy of Arianism or *ontological subordinationism*, which claims that the Son is not truly divine but is rather an exalted creature. That is, Arianism does not regard the persons as consubstantial or of the same essence or nature. So all views must maintain that the Son is truly God, and the same goes for the Holy Spirit. Another heresy to avoid is Sabellianism or *modalism*, which claims that the three divine persons are not really distinct persons; instead, a single person is playing three different roles. Finally, Christians must avoid *polytheism*, which says that there is more than one God. Christians must embrace monotheism.

As may be well known, some people have tried to make sense of claims (1)–(3) by positing overly simplistic analogies. Although some

---

8. For example, see Richard Cross, "Two Models of the Trinity?" *Heythrop Journal* 43 (2002): 275–94. See also Sarah Coakley, "Persons in the 'Social' Doctrine of the Trinity," in *The Trinity*, ed. Stephen T. Davis, Daniel Kendall, SJ, and Gerald O'Collins, SJ (Oxford: Oxford University Press, 1999).

modern theologians balk at the idea of providing any analogy for the triune God, historically it was fairly common to provide analogies to help make sense of what God is like—even while acknowledging that these analogies will be faulty because God is absolutely unique. However, in recent times, several popular analogies have become particularly problematic. For example, some say that the Trinity is like having one egg but also the yolk, the albumen, and the shell, which are three different things. But this analogy doesn't work since the yolk, albumen, and shell are not "of the same substance," and so this example falls afoul of Arianism (ontological subordinationism).

Another problematic analogy is saying that just as Stephen Curry is a Warrior, Klay Thompson is a Warrior, and Draymond Green is a Warrior, nevertheless, there is only one Warriors team. But this analogy does not avoid polytheism, especially since there are still three Warriors.

And you may have heard it taught that the Trinity is like some quantity of water that can be in three different states: ice, liquid, and vapor. Or similarly, a human being can play three different roles, such as being a mother, daughter, and sister. But these last two analogies fall prey to Sabellianism (modalism), since they involve a single person or object playing different roles, and so they fail to appreciate the distinctness or "threeness" of the persons. Many other problematic analogies have been offered, and they are to be rejected since they fail to avoid one of the heresies.

Our point is not to be negative but to help Christians realize how difficult it is to think about these issues; and so Christians need to proceed carefully, reflectively, openly, and most important of all, prayerfully. Looking for a quick and easy solution or analogy may lead to sloppy or lazy thinking, which can unwittingly lead to a heretical belief or to practical problems. We invite you to think slowly and carefully through some of the proposals that philosophical theologians have tried to offer. We encourage you to be critical of these accounts too, and perhaps even try to defend one of them, revise one of them, or come up with your own. Perhaps the more you study this doctrine, you will be able to come up with a better proposal, one that not only makes logical sense but also fits better with the teachings of Scripture. After focusing on several different approaches to understanding the doctrine of the Trinity, we will conclude by offering some suggestions for Christians as they reflect philosophically on this important doctrine.

The Latin Trinity

The Latin approach to the doctrine of the Trinity is based on Latin-speaking medieval philosophers, in particular Augustine and Aquinas. These theologians seem to have taken the oneness or unity of God as a starting point and then attempted to explain how there can be three persons. They frequently used psychological analogies to try to understand the doctrine of the Trinity. For example, Augustine suggested that the Trinity is like the mind, especially insofar as the mind can remember itself, understand itself, and also love itself. The remembering is akin to the Father, the self-understanding is akin to the Son, and the self-loving is akin to the Holy Spirit. In the end Augustine was not happy with this analogy nor with other psychological analogies he considered.

Another difficulty is that Augustine and most medieval philosophers accepted a strong version of the doctrine of divine simplicity, which claims that in God there are no parts, division, or complexity of any kind. So how could there be three of anything in God? Scripture seems to suggest that there are relations among the persons. God the Father begets God the Son. And God the Father and God the Son send God the Spirit.[9] Relations do not seem to be intrinsic features in a subject—they are what connect subjects together. Augustine thought that there are relations in God, such as the relation of begetting and proceeding. But because relations are not things or substances,

---

9. This claim led to a huge controversy between Western and Eastern Christians, a dispute over the *filioque* clause in the Nicene Creed. The original creed stated that the Spirit proceeded from the Father, but the Western pope appended the clause "and the Son" without the approval of other bishops, which (among many other reasons) led to the division between the Eastern church and the Western church in AD 1054.

a multiplicity of relations would not undermine God's simplicity. But Augustine took it a step further—he equated the divine persons with the relations, and therefore the divine persons do not add complexity to the divine nature in a way that would be problematic.

No doubt the strong version of the doctrine of divine simplicity as well as the identification of divine persons with relations are controversial theses, but several philosophical theologians accepted these views and built on them. For example, relations do not seem to be substantive enough to count as persons. Aware of this concern, Thomas Aquinas, the great medieval theologian, claimed that the divine persons are "subsistent relations"—relations that have their own way of existing like an individual. The concept of a *subsistent relation* is a hard one to unpack, and without surprise, this concept, too, is controversial. Some philosophers argue that such a concept makes no sense, for how could something be an individual and a relation at the same time? Others defend it and believe that it aids in thinking about the Trinity.

Our focus, however, is not on the historical development but on contemporary treatment. The most well-known contemporary Latin Trinitarian view tries to capture what Augustine and Aquinas were advancing, but it attempts to explain how a single self can have "three-ness" through an example of time travel.[10]

Imagine Jane, who is a dancer for the Rockettes. Suppose that she shows up to perform, but when she arrives, she realizes that she is the only one there. So she goes on and performs her routine. Afterward she goes into a back closet where there is a time-travel machine, and she sets the dial to one minute before the performance. When she gets out, she goes to the right of the dancing Rockette (which is Jane herself) and goes through the routine. After that performance she goes back into the time machine one more time and comes out again one minute before the performance. This time she goes to the left of the original dancing Rockette and goes through the routine. From the

10. The following account and example come from Brian Leftow, "A Latin Trinity," *Faith and Philosophy* 21 (2004): 304–33.

audience's perspective, there are three dancers, which we can name Left Rockette, Middle Rockette, and Right Rockette. These three dancers can acknowledge each other, talk to each other, and support each other in the routine. However, there is just one Jane living her life in these three different "streams." If this works, then it looks like we have a good model for the Trinity: one Jane and three dancing Rockettes, which is like one God and three divine persons.

How does this approach address the logical problem expressed in (1)–(3)? Suppose we replaced the relevant terms with Jane and the dancing Rockettes. Then we would say that Jane is the Left Rockette and Jane is the Right Rockette, and so the Left Rockette is the Right Rockette. Would claiming that "the Left Rockette is identical to the Right Rockette" be problematic? Well it depends. If we understand "Left Rockette" and "Right Rockette" descriptively (that is, "Left Rockette" means the Rockette on the left), then it is false, since they are different—one is on the left and the other is on the right. However, if we understand those terms to be what philosophers call *rigid designators* (which refers to Jane in whatever scenario, including nonactual ones), then the claim that the Left Rockette is the Right Rockette is unproblematic, since that is just to say, "Jane who is on the left side is identical to Jane who is on the right side."

Similar claims can be made with "Father" and "Son" (and "Spirit"). If we take these terms descriptively, then saying, "The Father is the Son," is false (since one is described as unbegotten, whereas the other is described as begotten). But if we understand these terms as rigid designators, then "the Father is the Son" is true but unproblematic, for it is just to say, "The God who lives in the Father-stream is identical to the God who lives in the Son-stream" (and similar treatment can be applied to "the Spirit"). So a contradiction cannot be generated from (1)–(3).

We must address some further considerations and potential concerns, however. First, time travel is philosophically puzzling, and there might be some paradoxes concerning time travel that need to be resolved before employing such a concept to make sense of the Trinity. Moreover, when applied to God, this concept seems to turn the divine persons into something like "streams." But persons are traditionally understood as substances or things (like cats or baseballs), which do not appear to be stream-like. Finally, it remains a question whether this view (along with other Latin Trinitarian views) actually avoids the heresy of Sabellianism or modalism, for one might construe the time-travel example as involving only a single person playing different roles (such as the one person Jane playing the role of three Rockettes), and thereby failing to adhere to the orthodox claim that there are three distinct divine persons. Hence, defenders of Latin Trinitarianism need to ensure that their view can maintain the claim that there are three distinct divine persons.

Other Latin Trinitarian approaches exist,[11] but much of the recent philosophical discussion has focused on social Trinitarianism, and so we turn our attention to that approach.

The Social Trinity

You and I are persons. What does it mean to be a person? Many thinkers today take it in large part to mean being self-conscious or being able to have self-reflective thoughts. It is being able to meaningfully think or use the first-person pronoun "I." If there are three persons, then there must be three things, each of which can think or say "I." God the Father says, "This is my Son, whom I love; with him I am well

---

11. A recent proposal that makes use of the concept of extended simples (where simples have no smaller parts, and they are extended—that is, they take up physical space) would count as another Latin approach to the Trinity. Imagine a simple object O that is extended across a spatial region. Suppose we divide that spatial region into three parts: s1, s2, and s3. O is located in s1, is located in s2, and is located in s3. But since O doesn't have any proper parts, the whole of O is located in each spatial region. Now we can take O to be analogous to the one God and O's occupation of s1, s2, and s3 to be analogous to the divine persons. O's being located in s1 is a different "thing" than O's being located in s2, and so they are different persons. But it is one and the same O located in both. This approach no doubt raises many questions, especially since several assumptions concerning extended simples are contentious (such as the nature of space or space-time, the nature of the location or occupation relation, etc.). For a more elaborate and precise treatment of this proposal, see Martin Pickup, "The Trinity and Extended Simples," *Faith and Philosophy* 33 (2016): 414–40.

pleased" (Matt. 3:17), and God the Son says, "I and the Father are one" (John 10:30). "I" in the first passage refers to the Father, and "I" in the second passage refers to the Son.

Social Trinitarianism takes the three divine persons as its starting point. The big question then is: How can there be only one God? For if the Father, the Son, and the Holy Spirit are each God, doesn't that make three Gods? In answer to this question, social Trinitarians typically claim that the relationship had by the three persons is so special and unique that it makes them count as one God. However, social Trinitarians do not all agree on what that relationship is supposed to be. We'll consider several proposals that have been offered concerning what that relationship is and how it makes the three persons count as one God.

Some theologians suggest that what makes the claim "there is one and only one God" true is the fact that only the Father, the Son, and the Holy Spirit have the essential properties of being God. An essential property is a characteristic or an attribute something *must* have in order to exist or to be the kind of thing it is. Many theologians think that attributes such as omnipotence (being all-powerful), omniscience (being all-knowing), moral perfection, and the like are essential properties of being God. The Father, the Son, and the Holy Spirit have these features essentially, and no other being has these features. So there is a uniqueness among the three divine persons from all other existing things insofar as they are the only ones who possess these attributes and who have them essentially. Since only the three divine persons have these features, this makes them count as one God. Other theologians highlight the fact that the three divine persons form a unique divine family or divine community of which no other existing thing is a member.

However, some worry that this is not enough to guarantee oneness or monotheism. Perhaps what more is needed is this: not only do the divine persons belong to a single family, but they also are in harmony with respect to their desires, motivations, goals, actions, and will. That is, they never disagree, and they never want to! Whatever the Father wants to do, the Son and the Spirit want to do as well. Thus, the three divine persons are not like the Greek gods of Mount Olympus, who are always squabbling and betraying each other. There is much more cohesiveness in the Christian God. Their perfect love for each other ensures they never go against each other and that they are always in agreement. Although there are three selves (three I's), the three divine persons function as one. Some even go so far as to claim that not only do the three divine persons never disagree, but that it is impossible for them to disagree. So it is the functional unity and the impossibility of tension between the persons that yield monotheism.

Other social Trinitarians think that the unifying relationship has to do with the "origination" relations. God the Father is *unbegotten*, but God the Father *begets* God the Son (as the creed states, "the Son is eternally begotten of the Father"). Moreover, the Holy Spirit *proceeds* from the Father and the Son (or perhaps from the Father and through the Son, depending on your theological background). No other person is begotten of the Father, and no other person proceeds from the Father and/through the Son. Moreover, these origination relations make the divine persons dependent on each other so that you cannot have the Father without the Son, nor the Son without the Father, nor the Spirit without the Father and the Son, nor the Father and the Son without the Spirit. They all need each other and cannot exist without each other. So all of the divine persons are mutually interdependent—if one did not exist, then neither would any of the others. But only the Father, the Son, and the Holy Spirit are mutually interdependent, whereas all other existing things could go out of existence and the three divine persons would remain intact. Given this unique relationship that holds among the three divine persons, some social Trinitarians argue that this is enough to maintain the unity of God, and so it can be truly asserted that there is one and only one God.

While these proposals have been offered to ensure oneness, you might be concerned that these relationships are not enough to ensure monotheism. Would these relationships between the Father, the Son, and the Holy Spirit, either taken by themselves or in combination, yield one God, or might polytheism still be lurking?

Here is one reason for worrying that these relationships would not be sufficient for ensuring monotheism.[12] Let us first begin with what appears to be a clear case of polytheism, the Greek pantheon of gods, such as Zeus, Hera, Ares, Athena, among many others. Greek religion is typically regarded as a version of polytheism. It is fairly obvious to understand why. First, they do not all have the same powers or abilities— some are stronger than others and some are craftier than others. In fact, there are some gods who are relatively weak and several others who are foolish and apparently doltish. Athena appears to be much wiser than Ares, and Zeus appears to be much stronger than Hera. So they do not all have the same attributes. Moreover, they often have wills set against one another. They frequently try to foil one another's plans, deceive one another, or one-up each other. They do not all have the same desires or goals, as some want to protect Odysseus and others want him to suffer. So clearly Zeus, Hera, and Athena are three gods, not one god.

Now recall the relationships we discussed earlier that are supposed to hold between the Father, the Son, and the Holy Spirit. And let us imagine that Zeus, Hera, and Athena all of a sudden had those exact relationships to each other. For example, imagine that Zeus, Hera, and Athena wound up with all the exact same attributes, so that Athena became as strong as Zeus, and Zeus became as crafty as Hera. Let us also suppose that they form a unique community of which no other existing thing belongs—they and they alone are the beings of Mount Olympus. Furthermore, let's imagine that they never disagree with one another and are always in agreement and in support of one another's plans and goals. Let's go a step further and say that they are also mutually interdependent in some way, so that if one does not exist, then the others could not exist either.

After imagining that these relationships are now had by Zeus, Hera,

---

12. For a similar criticism, see Michael Rea, "Polytheism and Christian Belief," *Journal of Theological Studies* 57 (2006): 133–48.

and Athena, should we say that they now comprise one God—that it would be true to assert that in Mount Olympus there is one and only one God? In our judgment such a cohort of gods would still count as polytheistic, and hence the relationships discussed are insufficient to ensure monotheism. No doubt some philosophical theologians will disagree, and so we leave it to readers to think through these social Trinitarian approaches.

Whether you think this objection is right or not, offering up these relationships is not the only strategy or approach that social Trinitarians can take. Other proposals have been offered, and we will discuss two other social Trinitarian views that attempt to uphold the oneness of God.

One such view is superficially similar to the unsatisfactory egg analogy insofar as it thinks of the divine persons as *parts* of God, but this part-whole approach to the Trinity purports to avoid the obvious errors we mentioned in the egg analogy. Consider the mythical creature Cerberus, which was described as a three-headed dog.[13] Each head has its own center of consciousness and its own perspective. One head could be looking at food and another head could be looking at a foe, and we can give each head a name: Larry, Moe, and Curly. Larry is a canine, Moe is a canine, and Curly is a canine; this is because they each have the genetic structure of being a canine. However, there is one and only one three-headed dog. So Larry is not identical to Cerberus, since Cerberus is three-headed whereas Larry is not.

Similarly, there is one and only one Trinitarian God, but in God there are three distinct centers of consciousness. The divine persons are not identical to God, for God is triune, but the Father is not triune (and neither is the Son nor the Spirit). Rather, each divine person is a part of the one God (in the way that Larry, Moe, and Curly are parts of Cerberus).[14] Unlike the egg example, this approach allows the three

---

13. For more on this approach, see J. P. Moreland and William Lane Craig, *Philosophical Foundations for a Christian Worldview* (Downers Grove, IL: InterVarsity Press, 2003).

14. To be fair, Craig's talk of "parts" may only be heuristic (and so may not want to interpret "the Father is God" as "the Father is a part of God"). Rather, what seems crucial for this proposal is that there is a single being with three centers of consciousness.

divine persons to have the same divine nature (just as Larry, Moe, and Curly have the same canine nature). So depending on how far one pushes the part-whole analogy, this view can be used to interpret claim (1) from earlier as stating the Father is a part of God, the Son is a part of God, and the Holy Spirit is a part of God. Moreover, they are all numerically distinct parts, and hence they can endorse (2). And it appears that they can maintain (3) since there is one and only one God who is composed of those three parts. So this view appears to show how all three claims can be held without contradiction. Moreover, it seems to say that the persons are related to the one God in a way that can't be mimicked by the Greek gods—for none of them are parts of some whole. Moreover, those who take this part-whole approach often combine it with the relationships mentioned earlier. So not only are the three divine persons parts of the one God, but the Father, Son, and Holy Spirit are also mutually interdependent, always in agreement, possess all the same essential divine attributes, and so on.

While a promising approach, we think there are serious concerns with this view. First, it is a bit strange to think of the Father, the Son, and the Spirit as parts of God. Of course the talk about "parts" may not be literal, but then further explanation is required. Moreover, we might think that in the Cerberus example there are four things that are canine: Larry, Moe, Curly, *and* Cerberus. Similarly, we might think that there are four divine things: the Father, the Son, the Holy Spirit, and God. So it may appear that we have a Quaternity instead of a Trinity.

In response to the last objection, defenders of this approach have affirmed that there are two different ways of being divine, one way for the divine persons and another way for God. This is, however, puzzling. Far more explanation will be required to explain what it even means for there to be two ways of being divine. Is one way more fundamental than the other, and if so, which is the more fundamental form of divinity? Or are there two equally fundamental ways of being divine, and if so, how does that work? So much more in the view needs to be explained.

One final social Trinitarian view is *perichoretic monotheism,* which has been defended by one of us. This view takes the idea of *perichoresis*—which is a Greek word meaning something like "mutual indwelling" or "interpenetration"—as central in the doctrine of the Trinity. The divine persons indwell each other, interpenetrate each other, fully contain each other, are fully open to each other, and so on. These are obviously metaphors. Some theologians have tried to expound or provide a deeper explanation of *perichoresis*, but it seems to us that *perichoresis* cannot be stripped of its metaphorical aspect. That is because it is a way for us to talk about the triune God, who is utterly unique and cannot be wholly grasped by our limited minds. The three divine persons are really distinct; there are three different persons who can meaningfully think or say "I." We can illustrate this geometrically as three circles that do not overlap:

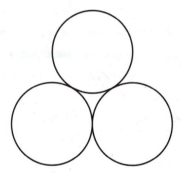

But by *perichoresis*, the three divine persons interpenetrate each other or are fully contained by each other. Following the geometric example, we might represent the three circles as overlapping so as to "contain" each other, as pictured below:

This looks like a single circle, but this figure is supposed to represent the three circles completely overlapping or circumscribing the same region. *Perichoresis*, according to some philosophers, is the divine persons being in some way like the first diagram and in some way like the second diagram. The first diagram clearly depicts threeness, and the second diagram clearly depicts oneness. So if the Father, the Son, and the Holy Spirit are perichoretically related to each other, then we can truly assert that there is one God.

This view has several upshots. First, it does not require saying that the divine persons are parts of God. Second, it explains why Zeus, Hera, and Athena are distinct gods even if they have the same attributes, always agree, and depend on each other for their existence, for the Greek gods are not perichoretically related to each other. But the Father, Son, and Spirit are, and so there is one God. Moreover, perichoretic monotheism need not claim that there are two ways of being divine. So this approach avoids several of the objections raised against the other versions of social Trinitarianism. In our view, perichoretic monotheism is the most plausible version of social Trinitarianism (though, for full disclosure, only one of us actually endorses this view).

A question will naturally arise of how something can be in both of the states depicted in both diagrams at the same time. We would typically say that it is impossible for anything to do so, and hence we would want an explanation for how it is even possible. In response, *perichoresis* was posited not to explain how it works; rather, it only tells us how we should think about the Trinity, which is akin to something being in both states simultaneously. Perhaps it is similar to what some quantum physicists tell us about light. Light has some features that make it appear as though it is comprised of particles, but it has other features that make it appear as though it is a wave. But particles are not waves, and it is hard to see how something can be both. This analogy is of course imperfect since physicists do try to offer models for how light can satisfy both sets of features, but the point of the example is that the appeal to *perichoresis* can retain much of the mystery of the Trinity while trying to allow for the true assertion that there are three divine persons and one God. If this approach is right, it appears that monotheism is guaranteed because it insists that the perichoretic relation between the Father, the Son, and the Holy Spirit automatically rules out polytheism.

However, perichoretic monotheism appears to ensure that there is no contradiction in (1)–(3) by sacrificing intelligibility; there is no explanation of *how* it works. Some philosophical theologians will be willing to embrace this element of mystery in a philosophical model of the Trinity. Again, no one doubts that the Trinity is a mystery, and no one thinks that the doctrine of the Trinity will be fully comprehensible to human minds. But critics of this view may be concerned that not enough has been explained in appealing to *perichoresis* and so is too unintelligible to count as a satisfactory model of the Trinity.

Latin Trinitarianism and social Trinitarianism have been approaches to the doctrine of the Trinity that stick with what we might call the standard understanding of the identity relation (=). However, philosophers have offered other ways of thinking about identity as well as other ways of thinking about logical concepts, and some philosophical theologians have employed these nonstandard concepts in order to develop a coherent theory of the Trinity. We examine one such approach next.

Relative Identity

When we say, "Clark Kent is the same person as Superman," philosophers have typically understood that sentence to mean that Clark Kent is a person, that Superman is a person, and that Clark Kent and Superman are identical. So identity here is being understood in an absolute sense—it is not qualified. So the idea of "sameness" isn't different when we talk about persons or cats or chairs or whatever. There is just identity: $a = a$. But some people think that identity is not absolute, that when we talk about sameness, it depends on the kind or sort of thing we are talking about. That is, identity is *relative* to a particular kind or sort. So cat-sameness might be different than chair-sameness.

Whenever we talk about identity or sameness, then, under this view, we have to specify which kind or sort of thing we are discussing.[15]

Let's talk about it abstractly first. For someone who accepts relative identity, it is possible for the following to all be asserted truly:

    i. x is A,

    ii. x is B,

    iii. y is A,

    iv. y is B,

    v. x is the same A as y, and

    vi. x is not the same B as y.

So although x and y are both A and B, they are the same A-thing but not the same B-thing. Let's now put this concretely with the Trinity. We can say that the Father is God and that the Father is a divine person. We can also say that the Son is God and that the Son is a divine person. And we can say that the Father is the same God as the Son. And given the last claim, we can say that the Father is not the same divine person as the Son. So by employing the concept of relative identity, we get the desired conclusion that the Father and the Son are not the same person while also being the same God (and the same goes for the Spirit—same God, different person). Relative identity, then, appears to be very useful when it comes to thinking about the Trinity.

One concern for this approach, however, is with its employment of relative identity. Some philosophers worry about the very concept of relative identity, claiming that identity can be understood only in the standard, absolute way. Moreover, others are concerned that the only thing that relative identity would be useful for is in understanding God. But if it doesn't apply to anything else in the world, then using relative identity in a theory would be *ad hoc*, meaning that we have no

---

15. Stronger relative identity views deny that there is absolute identity; however, weaker relative identity views keep absolute identity but claim that relative identity is not reducible to absolute identity but is rather a fundamental notion.

independent reason to accept it other than that it helps us solve our logical problem (and this would be a form of special pleading).

Some philosophical theologians do think, however, that relative identity is defensible and applicable even to other things besides God.[16] To show one way in which this might be done, let's suppose that we have a clay statue in front of us. It would be a normal reaction to say that there is only one thing in front of us, the statue made out of clay. However, a philosophical puzzle arises. Suppose that the clay statue was created out of a lump of clay on Tuesday, so that on Monday there was no statue but only a lump of clay. Moreover, we can imagine a steamroller coming by on Wednesday and flattening the statue. We would want to say that the statue no longer exists on Wednesday, but the lump of clay still does, for lumps of clay can survive being reshaped into different configurations. But if two things are identical, then any feature true of one is true of the other (this law of identity is sometimes called the *indiscernibility of identicals*). But since the lump of clay existed Monday and the statue did not, and since the lump of clay could survive flattening on Wednesday but the statue could not, they have different features. Therefore, we should conclude that the lump of clay and the statue are not identical to each other. So it appears we must say that there are two objects in front of us!

However, some argue that the lump of clay and the statue are united in some way so that we can still truly assert that there is a single material object in front of us—after all, we didn't initially think that there were two material objects in front of us when standing in front of the clay statue. We might count them as one material object since the statue and the lump of clay are made up of all the same matter. However, the lump of clay and the statue have different forms or structures, for the statue form doesn't allow it to be flattened, but the lump of clay's form does. Thus, the lump of clay and the statue can be analyzed as a form-matter compound (which is a view known as

---

16. Jeffrey Brower and Michael Rea, "Material Constitution and the Trinity," *Faith and Philosophy* 22 (2005): 57–76.

hylomorphism, from Greek *hylē*, "matter," and *morphē* "form," which goes all the way back to Aristotle). The lump of clay and the statue have different forms, and so they are not identical. However, they are both made up of the same matter, and hence there is only one material object. For if we count material objects by sameness of matter, we can say that the lump of clay and the statue are numerically the same (we count only one thing), but they are not identical to each other because they have different forms. Proponents of this view, then, allow for another sameness relation besides identity, so that two things can be the same A-thing (material object) but distinct B-things (hylomorphic compounds).

Now this solution to the philosophical puzzle can be applied to God. This view would analyze the divine persons as form-matter compounds. But of course God is not a material thing and so has no matter. However, we can think of something that plays the role of matter. In God's case it would be the divine essence. The Father, the Son, and the Holy Spirit all have the same divine essence. However, the divine persons each have a different form—perhaps their own personal properties or their own unique relational status (fatherhood, sonship, etc.). Since they have different forms, the divine persons are distinct hylomorphic (matter-form) compounds, and so the Father, the Son, and the Holy Spirit are not identical to each other, which is claim (2). Moreover, they each have the same divine essence, which is claim (1). And in virtue of having the same divine essence, they count as the same God, which is claim (3). Hence, this form-matter approach to the Trinity allows for a consistent way of accepting (1)–(3) without falling into contradiction.

As with most philosophical positions, this approach is not without criticism. This particular version of a form-matter view still appeals to relative identity, so some of the criticisms for the earlier version might be applicable here. Others fear that this view captures the wrong relation between the divine persons to each other or the wrong relation between the divine persons to the divine essence. Our own assessment is that the view would be made more plausible with certain significant modifications, where the spirit of the hylomorphic approach is retained but without appeal to another sameness relation besides identity (for we both believe there is only one fundamental sameness relation, namely, absolute identity). Whether we should use a standard notion of identity or instead employ relative identity remains unsettled among philosophers and philosophical theologians.

CONCLUDING THOUGHTS

We'll briefly give our own assessment of the theories surveyed here. We are worried about relative identity approaches, including the hylomorphic variant that appeals to numerical sameness without identity. This is not primarily because of theological concerns but because of our metaphysical view—in particular that the fundamental relation of identity is absolute and not relative to kinds or sorts. Of the social Trinitarian views, we regard perichoretic monotheism as the most plausible of the versions because it best avoids the error of polytheism; however, we recognize that it retains quite a bit of mystery in explaining the logical possibility of maintaining (1)–(3). And we are sympathetic with some versions of Latin Trinitarianism, but much more needs to be explained and defended. Some recent work on the logic of parts (and wholes) and the metaphysics of location has led to fruitful advances in philosophical discussions,[17] and we think that further exploration in these areas can produce advances in Trinitarian theorizing. While these theories are fairly novel, some of them do have historical precedence, and so such theorizing is best approached by joining with the efforts of historical theologians.

One worry we have for readers is the feeling of discouragement insofar as there is no agreed upon way of making sense of (1)–(3),

---

17. For example, see A. J. Cotnoir, "Mutual Indwelling," *Faith and Philosophy* 34 (2017): 123–51.

especially since we raised concerns and criticisms for each of the views that have been examined in this chapter. However, we hope that you are not discouraged in the least. What this work shows is that Christians have sought to assess and defend the logical coherence of the doctrine of the Trinity. Superficial or quick dismissals of the doctrine of the Trinity by those who claim it leads to a contradiction can be addressed without fear. Christians have been thinking about this doctrine for a long time, and many Christian philosophical theologians believe that it can be rationally defended in the sense that it doesn't lead to any contradiction. However, none of the views examined is required for orthodoxy, and none is perfect or without objection. Perhaps that is what we should expect on this side of death. The Trinity is, as we have been reiterating time and time again, a mystery that will never be fully comprehended by human beings in this life. The goal of the philosophical theologian, then, is not to show definitively that there is no mystery but to show that a contradiction is not contained in the doctrine. Which theory provides the correct model? Perhaps we will never know until we see God face-to-face.

Such tentative conclusions may also make some people not want to bother spending time reflecting on the doctrine of the Trinity. As we said in the introduction, however, we are people who start with faith—but our faith commitments have led to several questions, and so our faith seeks after understanding. Accordingly, such theorizing is not a waste of time. Such reflections have apologetic value insofar as it helps us to address and respond to objections against the doctrine of the Trinity. Moreover, such theorizing is also spurred on by love. The more you love someone, the more you want to know all the details about that person, even if that person is psychologically and emotionally complex. It is out of our love of God that we want to know more about him, especially as he has revealed himself to us as triune.

So, as you think about these ideas, here are several things all Christians should keep in mind when reflecting on the doctrine of the Trinity:

- First, any view must not conflict with what we learn in Scripture about God.
- Second, views should, as much as possible, adhere to the creedal statements that have been accepted by most Christians.
- Third, any view should be able to explain how it avoids the major heresies or errors.
- Fourth, one's view should not be dismissive of the spiritual and practical importance of the Trinity. Discussion of the Trinity is not merely to engage in abstract theorizing. Our worship and prayer life should be properly framed by our understanding of the triune God.
- Fifth, we need to be open-minded, with a willingness to be shown when we are or might be wrong. Hence, theologians need to listen to philosophers, and philosophers need to listen to theologians. Pastors need to listen to Christian academics, and Christian academics need to listen to pastors. Trinitarian reflection must be an effort of the whole church.
- Finally, we need to be constantly praying, interacting with the triune God to enlighten our minds through the wisdom that comes to us through the Holy Spirit.

Although this kind of philosophical reflection might be daunting given the logical rigor, we can say from experience that such reflection can deepen love for God, who is mysterious but who has also revealed himself to us.

FURTHER READINGS

For arguments that aim to prove why there must be a plurality in God, see Stephen T. Davis, "A Somewhat Playful Proof of the Social Trinity in Five Easy Steps," *Philosophia Christi* 1 (1999):103–5. For a substantive treatment of the different views, see Michael Rea's entry

"The Trinity" in *The Oxford Handbook of Philosophical Theology*, ed. Thomas Flint and Michael Rea (Oxford: Oxford University Press, 2011); and Harriet Baber's "The Trinity" in the Internet Encyclopedia of Philosophy, www.iep.utm.edu/trinity/. For Latin Trinitarianism, see Brian Leftow, "A Latin Trinity," *Faith and Philosophy* 21 (2004): 304–33. For social Trinitarianism, a substantive treatment can be found in Richard Swinburne, *The Christian God* (Oxford: Clarendon, 1994). For an elaboration of the Cerberus example and the part/whole approach, see the relevant chapter in J. P. Moreland and William Lane Craig, *Philosophical Foundations for a Christian Worldview* (Downers Grove, IL: InterVarsity Press, 2003). For more on *perichoresis*, see Stephen T. Davis, "Perichoretic Monotheism," in *Christian Philosophical Theology* (Oxford: Oxford University Press, 2006). For the relative identity view, see Peter van Inwagen, "Three Persons in One Being," in *The Trinity: East/West Dialogue*, ed. Melville Y. Stewart; trans. Eugene Grushetsky and Xenia Grushetsky (Dordrecht: Springer Science & Business Media, 2003); and Jeffrey Brower and Michael Rea, "Material Constitution and the Trinity," *Faith and Philosophy* 22 (2005): 487–505, which discusses the statue/lump case that employs numerical sameness without identity.

For excellent philosophical discussion on the doctrine of the Trinity, which also includes substantive historical discussion, see William Hasker, *Metaphysics and the Tri-Personal God* (Oxford: Oxford University Press, 2017); Thomas H. McCall, *Which Trinity? Whose Monotheism? Philosophical and Systematic Theologians on the Metaphysics of Trinitarian Theology* (Grand Rapids: Eerdmans, 2010); and Stephen T. Davis, Daniel Kendall, SJ, and Gerald O'Collins, SJ, eds., *The Trinity* (Oxford: Oxford University Press, 2004).

THE INCARNATION

C hristians believe in an incarnate God, that God became man. More specifically, we believe that the second person of the Trinity, God the Son, became a human being. Jesus Christ was clearly human: he was born, he breathed, he ate, and he slept. But he was also divine. He received worship from his disciples and forgave sins that were not committed directly against him, but only God should be worshiped and only God can forgive sins not directly committed against oneself.

In this chapter we will focus on several theories of the incarnation. However, there are other philosophical questions that arise when reflecting on the fact that God became man. One very obvious question is: Why? Why would God become incarnate? Some claim that God had to do it given his aim to save humanity. Others think that God could have reconciled human beings in other ways but that the incarnation is the most fitting (or makes the most sense) given God's aim in saving human beings along with other contingent features of the world that God created. And some theologians have argued that the atonement could only be accomplished by a person who was both God and human (and we will discuss the atonement in depth in chapter 5). While these questions are extremely interesting, we will focus on the so-called logical problem of the incarnation, which is sometimes referred to as the "fundamental problem of Christology." We will look at proposals that try to make sense of how one and the same person can be both divine and human. That said, let us first turn to the question of why Christians have historically believed that Christ is divine. The main reason is usually the revelation of such a claim in Scripture and tradition, especially in the creeds. However, some philosophers both historically and now have offered philosophical arguments for the divinity of Christ.

BELIEVING IN CHRIST'S DIVINITY

According to John 1, "In the beginning was the Word, and the Word was with God, and the Word was God. . . . The Word became flesh and made his dwelling among us. We have seen his glory, the glory of the one and only Son, who came from the Father, full of grace and truth" (vv. 1, 14). This passage indicates that Christ is the Word who was with God and who was God, and that this Word became flesh, namely, a human being. And in 1 Corinthians 8:6, Paul stated that "for us there is but one God, the Father, from whom all things came and for whom we live; and there is but one Lord, Jesus Christ, through whom all things came and through whom we live." Many interpreters believe that Paul used "Lord" (Gk., *kyrios*) as the expression for the divine name of God (the tetragrammaton), and hence there appears to be some indication that Christ is in some sense divine. There are of course many hermeneutical and historical nuances and complications here, and we leave it to biblical exegetes and historical theologians to assess these texts properly. But in our estimation, the view that Christ was not only human but also divine best explains the data we have in the texts of the New Testament.

Belief in Christ as divine and human was also affirmed at the Council of Chalcedon in 451. At this time many different views were held regarding *what* Christ was (metaphysically speaking), and many such views were deemed as heresies. Here is an excerpt of the so-called Chalcedonian Definition accepted at the council:

> We, then, following the holy fathers, all with one consent, teach men to confess one and the same Son, our Lord Jesus Christ, the

same perfect in Godhead and also perfect in manhood; truly God and truly man, of a reasonable soul and body; consubstantial with the Father according to the Godhead, and consubstantial with us according to the Manhood . . . one and the same Christ, Son, Lord, Only-begotten, to be acknowledged in two natures, inconfusedly, unchangeably, indivisibly, inseparably; the distinction of natures being by no means taken away by the union, but rather the property of each nature being preserved, and concurring in one Person and one Subsistence, not parted or divided into two persons, but one and the same Son.[1]

It should be noted that this does not give us a definition in the philosophical sense of a definition. Nor does it give us an actual account or theory of the incarnation. Rather, many scholars agree that the Chalcedonian Definition merely provides the boundaries of an orthodox view of the incarnation—that is, it must be maintained that there is one person with two natures, where the natures are not confused and the person is not divided.

At another ecumenical council, the Third Council of Constantinople, it was declared that in Christ there were two distinct wills: a divine will and a human will (which is called *dyothelitism*). While historically most theories of the incarnation have tried to maintain this claim, some Christian thinkers do not recognize the authority of this particular conciliar pronouncement and so have felt free to reject dyothelitism—accepting instead that there is one will in Christ (*monothelitism*). We will not get into this debate but merely note that dyothelitism, while a traditional claim, is not universally accepted by all Christian thinkers who provide models of the incarnation.

Some Christian thinkers have also offered philosophical arguments to defend the claim that Christ is divine. Perhaps the most well-known

---

1. Chalcedonian Definition, *Creeds of Christendom*, vol. 2, ed. Philip Schaff, Christian Classics Ethereal Library, www.ccel.org/ccel/schaff/creeds2.iv.i.iii.html.

version is the Mad, Bad, God argument, which is sometimes referred to as the Lord, Liar, or Lunatic argument. While this argument may be traced back to Pascal, its most well-known presentation was offered by C. S. Lewis, an Oxford and Cambridge scholar whose fame is primarily based on his fictional and apologetic works, such as the Chronicles of Narnia and *Mere Christianity*. Some contemporary philosophers and apologists have endorsed the argument. In brief, the Mad, Bad, God argument can be formulated as follows:

> The Scriptures teach that Jesus Christ claimed either explicitly or implicitly to be divine through his life, teaching, and actions (see John 10:30–38 and Mark 2:5–10). Either his claim was true or it was not. If his claim was false, then Jesus either knew it was false or he did not know it was false. Now, if he knew it was false, then he is lying and deceiving others around him to believe falsely that he was something that he wasn't—so he was morally bad. But if he didn't know his claim was false, then he should be regarded as a lunatic, for usually people who claim to be divine (when they aren't) are not right in the head—and so he was mentally mad. But many individuals believe that Jesus was at bare minimum a good moral prophet, one that was rational and lucid of mind. So Jesus was neither morally bad nor mentally mad—i.e., he was neither a liar nor a lunatic. So the only other alternative is that his claim was true; thus, Jesus truly was divine.[2]

However, some criticisms have been raised against this argument. For example, one might agree that Christ was neither mad nor bad yet argue that the Gospels are not historically reliable, and so the claims to divinity by Jesus are legendary or fictional. Hence, a full

---

2. For more on this argument, see Stephen T. Davis, "Was Jesus Mad, Bad, or God?" in *The Incarnation*, ed. Stephen T. Davis, Daniel Kendall, SJ, and Gerald O'Collins, SJ (Oxford: Oxford University Press 2002), 221–45.

defense of this argument requires defending the historical reliability of the New Testament and the claim that the Gospels really do depict Jesus as claiming to be divine, whether implicitly or explicitly. Others have argued that even if Christ was neither mad nor bad, he may have been sincerely mistaken.[3] One could imagine a nondivine figure who had qualitatively indiscernible experiences as Christ, such that this nondivine figure had all the same evidence as Christ did, and so would reasonably believe he is divine when in fact he is mistaken. However, we think that the "sincerely mistaken" option is extremely difficult to hold given an understanding of how a first-century Palestinian Jew living in that particular contextual milieu might make such claims to divinity without being either insane or wicked.

Another argument for the divinity of Christ is connected to the case for the resurrection. For example, some argue that a strong historical case can be made for the fact of Christ's resurrection from the dead (usually based on the claim that the best explanation of certain facts—such as an empty tomb, resurrection appearances, and the transformed character of the disciples—is the fact that Christ rose from the dead). Given the meaning of the resurrection in the particular context of Christ's life and mission, some philosophers argue that the probability of the resurrection increases the probability that the incarnation occurred (and similarly, the incarnation makes it more likely that the resurrection occurred—and so both events support each other).[4]

So if these arguments are successful, then Christians have reason to believe that Jesus Christ is divine. However, even if these arguments fail, the main impetus for accepting Christ's divinity is special revelation, especially in Scripture and in the creeds.

---

3. Daniel Howard-Snyder, "Was Jesus Mad, Bad, or God? . . . or Merely Mistaken?" *Faith and Philosophy* 21 (2004): 456–79.

4. For detailed treatment of this argument, see Richard Swinburne, *The Resurrection of God Incarnate* (Oxford: Oxford University Press, 2003).

AVOIDING HERESIES

Similar to the doctrine of the Trinity, adherence to the traditional doctrine of the incarnation requires avoiding certain errors, especially if one accepts the Chalcedonian Definition. Here is a list of several heresies that were rejected either at Chalcedon or at other Christian councils:

> **DOCETISM:** God the Son did not really become human but merely appeared as though he did.
>
> **MONOPHYSITISM:** Christ had only a single nature, either just the divine nature or some combination, such as a *theanthropic* (God-man) nature.
>
> **ARIANISM:** Jesus was not really divine but was merely a very special and exalted creature of God.
>
> **APOLLINARIANISM:** God did not take on a human soul or mind but only a human body.
>
> **NESTORIANISM:** There are really two persons in Christ, a human person and a divine person.

Contra docetism, early Christian leaders maintained that Christ had a genuine physical body. Contra monophysitism, they claimed that Christ had two distinct natures. Contra Arianism, they believed that Christ was consubstantial—that is, he had the same essence or nature—with God the Father. Contra Apollinarianism, they maintained that Christ's human nature was comprised of both a human soul and a human body. And contra Nestorianism, there is only one person in Christ. So traditional Christianity has kept the following formula of the incarnation: Christ is *one person* with *two natures*.

But similar to the doctrine of the Trinity, we appear to get into a "counting" problem: how can one person have two different natures? So we turn next to the main logical puzzle pertaining to the doctrine of the incarnation.

THE LOGICAL PROBLEM

Similar to our previous discussion of the Trinity, there are some concerns over an apparent logical incoherence in the formula. Some take the quick response that there is no contradiction since Christians are saying that there is one *person* and two *natures*. If Christians claimed that there is one person and two persons, or one nature and two natures, then that would be a blatant contradiction. However, even a more nuanced examination of common Christian commitments appears to lead to a contradiction. Here are some of those commitments:

(1) Jesus is divine.

(2) Jesus is human.

(3) Every divine being is omniscient (all-knowing), omnipotent (all-powerful), eternal, and immaterial (among other attributes).

(4) Every human being is limited in power, limited in knowledge, temporal (exists in time), and embodied.

But by (1)–(4), it seems that we are committed to claiming that Jesus is both omniscient and not omniscient, which appears to be impossible. How can someone know everything and not know everything at the same time? Maybe being human does not require being limited in knowledge. But Jesus is portrayed as being limited in knowledge, especially when he states that he does not know the hour of his return but that only the Father knows (Matt. 24:36), and one of the Gospels reports that Jesus "grew in wisdom" (Luke 2:52), which does not seem like something an omniscient being can do. This apparent contradiction in the doctrine of the incarnation (as expressed in (1)–(4)) is often called by philosophers "the fundamental problem of Christology."

So there appears to be a logical incoherence in the doctrine of the incarnation, for something cannot be both omniscient and not omniscient, but Christ appears to be omniscient given his divine nature and not omniscient given his human nature. Obviously the logical tension goes beyond just omniscience and being limited in knowledge. If Christ is divine, then he is omnipotent; but if he is also human, then he is limited in power. God is also incorporeal, which means that God does not have a body, and yet humans have a body, so Jesus is both bodily and not bodily. Some claim that God is unchanging, and yet human beings are changing, so Jesus is both changing and unchanging. And therefore, many of the divine attributes and human attributes can form a pair, where no single being is able to have both attributes simultaneously. So how can these contradictions be avoided? And remember, contradiction must be avoided while also avoiding the above mentioned heresies.

Although Christians traditionally affirm that Jesus is God and human, there is no official statement or position regarding *how* this might work. So Christian thinkers throughout church history and even now have tried to offer accounts that yield a coherent doctrine while remaining faithful to the teachings of the Bible and the early creeds and councils (such as the Apostles' Creed, the Nicene Creed, the Chalcedonian Definition, etc.). Similar to our discussion of the Trinity, we will present several positions that have been offered to make sense of the incarnation. Again, these views do not exhaust all the options, but we offer these as a representation of how philosophical theologians approach the charge of logical incoherence regarding the doctrine of the incarnation.

The "Qua" Approach

A traditional approach of trying to solve this concern is to claim that there is one way that Jesus is omniscient and another way that Jesus is not omniscient. After all, Jesus's omniscience is connected to his divinity, and his limited knowledge is connected to his humanity. So this strategy claims that *as God*, Jesus is omniscient, but *as human*, Jesus is not omniscient. That is, we cannot merely predicate to Jesus various attributes; they must be appropriately *qualified*. This approach became widely used by medieval theologians, who sometimes used a "qua" modifier in Latin to make the necessary qualifications clearer.

So when the claim is made that Jesus is omnipotent and Jesus is not omnipotent, it must be qualified as follows:

(Qua-D)   Jesus is omnipotent *qua* being divine.

(Qua-H)   Jesus is not omnipotent *qua* being human.

But how exactly are we to understand the "qua being divine" and the "qua being human" expressions? Philosophical theologians have interpreted (Qua-D) and (Qua-H) in several different ways.

One natural way to interpret (Qua-D) and (Qua-H) is to say that what the "qua" clause is doing is explaining why something is true of Jesus. So we might understand "Jesus is omnipotent qua being divine" as saying that Jesus is omnipotent *in virtue of* being divine or *because of* his divinity. So Jesus's divinity explains why he is omnipotent, and his humanity explains why he is not omnipotent. We might make this interpretation explicit by formulating the two claims as:

(Qua-D1)   Qua-being divine: Jesus is omnipotent.

(Qua-H1)   Qua-being human: Jesus is not omnipotent.

Interpreting the "qua" expressions in this way has been called the *reduplicative approach* to the fundamental problem.

While the reduplicative approach has a superficial appearance of resolving the problem, with a bit more reflection, it should be evident why it does not do so. For example, we can say that *qua–being a professor*, Eric has students, and *qua–being a dad*, Eric has children. That is, what explains Eric having students is being a professor, and what explains Eric having children is being a dad. But that implies that Eric has students and children. So saying "qua–being divine, Jesus is omniscient" and "qua–being human, Jesus is not omniscient" implies that Jesus is omniscient and not omniscient—which leads us back to our contradiction. So the reduplicative strategy does not solve the fundamental problem of Christology.

Perhaps we can nuance it a bit, as many medieval theologians did. Perhaps what is meant is the following:

(Qua-D2) Jesus-qua-God is omniscient.
(Qua-H2) Jesus-qua-human is not omniscient.

That is, the "qua" operates on the subject and not on the entire assertion. But what does saying "Jesus-qua-God" and "Jesus-qua-human" mean? One common way to interpret this is to say that Jesus Christ is made up of parts. He has a God-part and a human-part, and that human-part is typically construed as being comprised of a human soul and a human body. So, before the incarnation, there was only the God-part in Christ. But after the incarnation, there was the God-part plus the human-part (soul + body), and Jesus Christ is the person made up of both parts (or more precisely, three parts: the divine nature, the human soul, and the human body).

On this view, Jesus's God-part is omniscient and Jesus's human-part is not omniscient. So this version of the "qua" approach avoids having to claim that one and the same thing is both omniscient and not omniscient in exactly the same way, which would yield a contradiction. Instead, Jesus is omniscient because he has a part that is omniscient, and Jesus is not omniscient because he has a part that is not omniscient. This is like saying that someone has a scar because she has a part, say her foot, that has a scar.

This was a strategy that several medieval theologians such as Aquinas appeared to favor. Contradiction can be avoided because the incompatible properties—omniscience and limited knowledge—are not strictly possessed by the exact same thing; rather, they are possessed by different parts of Christ.

But even this approach comes with a few questions and concerns. One worry is that it is a bit strange to say that God the Son can "grow" in parts, and it is hard to explain exactly how that is supposed to work. Did God the Son start out with one part and then add two more parts, the human soul and the human body? But this raises a puzzle. Suppose we have God the Son prior to the incarnation, and since Christians think that Christ preexisted the incarnation, it is common to suppose that God the Son is identical to Christ. God the Son, prior to the incarnation, has a single part, namely, the God-part. Since that is the only part he has prior to the incarnation, it is natural to claim that God the Son is identical to the God-part.[5] At the incarnation, the God-part is conjoined with a human soul and a human body. At the incarnation, then, Christ is composed of the God-part, the human soul, and the human body. But we earlier stated that Christ is identical to God the Son, and God the Son is identical to the God-part. So we are forced to claim that Christ is identical to the God-part. But that conflicts with the claim that Christ has more than the God-part; he also has the human soul and the human body. So a puzzle exists over the manner in which Christ can acquire parts if Christ is identical to God the Son.

Perhaps the way to avoid this problem is to claim that while God the Son is identical to the divine nature, God the Son is not identical to Jesus Christ, since God the Son has only one part, the God-part, whereas Christ has three parts, the God-part, the human soul, and the human body. So the relation of God the Son and Christ is not identity but parthood—God the Son is a (proper) part of Christ.

But this answer is a bit worrisome as well, for God the Son is a person, and there is only one divine person in Christ, as the Council of Chalcedon and Scripture claim. But Christ would not count as a person if God the Son is a person; or God the Son is not a person if Christ is. Both of these claims are strange, for what would Christ be if not a person? And God the Son was at least a person before the incarnation; so why wouldn't God the Son be a person after the incarnation?

---

5. Philosophers often distinguish between improper parthood and proper parthood. If x is a proper part of y, then x is not identical to y. Moreover, many think that if x is a proper part of y, then there must be some other part of y that is distinct from x. Improper parts are just the wholes themselves—that is, everything is an improper part of itself. So when philosophers use the term *part*, it often is ambiguous between proper and improper parthood. The ordinary usage of *part* seems to match up fairly closely with the notion of proper parthood.

Additionally, general concerns have been raised over using talk of parts when trying to understand the incarnation.

This "God-part, human-part" approach has been defended from these concerns that have been raised against it, and you should think for yourself whether talking about parts in an account of the incarnation is useful or problematic. But the reduplicative approach and the subject-modification approach have not been the only ways of taking a qua approach to the incarnation. Other philosophical theologians suggest that we should reinterpret the qua approach so that it applies to the predicates. That is, we can construe the qua approach as:

> (Qua-D3) Christ is omniscient qua-being-divine.
> (Qua-H3) Christ is not omniscient qua-being-human.

This interpretation appears to avoid a contradiction, unlike the reduplicative approach. And it does not require talking about parts to make sense of the incarnation.

But the concern with applying the "qua" on the predicates is in even trying to figure out what those qualities are supposed to mean or to understand their metaphysical natures. What is the difference between omniscience and omniscience-qua-divinity? And what is the difference between being limited in knowledge and being limited-in-knowledge-qua-humanity? Moreover, the Christian tradition claims that Christ took on a human nature and so is like us human beings in every way except for sin. It is true of humans like us that we are limited in knowledge, *full stop*. But this view claims that Christ does not have the property of being limited in knowledge, period, but rather has the property of being limited in knowledge-qua-humanity. This appears to be a different property. So, then, Christ has different properties than we do, and so this approach has difficulty in claiming that Christ shares the same kind of human nature as we do.

We have provided several different interpretations of the *qua* approach to the incarnation. There are other ways of employing *qua*—for example, it may apply to the copula, the "is" in the statement (that is, "Christ is-qua-divinity omniscient" and "Christ is-qua-humanity not omniscient"), though even this proposal runs into serious problems.

We think that the reduplicative approach and the view that takes the "qua" to apply to predicates are too problematic and so should be rejected on the basis of the concerns raised above. We do think that the approach that applies the "qua" operator on the subject is the most promising version, though much more work on the logic of parthood and its application to the incarnation must be developed in order to provide a plausible view.

Two-Minds View

Instead of talking about parts or using a *qua* modifier, one recent approach to the incarnation focuses instead on contemporary psychological concepts. Probably the most well-known version is to claim that in Jesus Christ there are "two minds" or two distinct ranges of consciousness.[6] One mind is omniscient and so knows everything there is to know, but the other mind is not omniscient and knows whatever a typical human growing up in first-century Palestine would know (but he is clearly highly intelligent and wise). So when Jesus claimed not to know who touched him (Luke 8:45), this was the human mind speaking, though the divine mind knew exactly who touched him. Everything the human mind knows, the divine mind knows; but the human mind does not know everything the divine mind knows. We might loosely state that the human mind is contained in the divine mind, but the divine mind is not contained in the human mind.

Obviously the divine mind's ability to know everything the human mind knows is not going to be sufficient to account for the unity of the two natures of Christ. This should be evident because God is omniscient, and so God knows everything that *every* human mind knows, not just the human mind of Christ. God also knows everything

---

6. Thomas Morris, *The Logic of God Incarnate* (Ithaca, NY: Cornell University Press, 1986).

you know and we know. But we are not united to God the Son in the way the human nature of Christ is supposed to be. So there needs to be a tighter relation between the two minds. What has typically been appealed to is the relation of the divine will and the human will in Christ (and so the two-minds view fits nicely with *dyothelitism*). For normal human beings, our wills are somewhat autonomous and not ordinarily overridden by God—though God could override our wills at any time. But according to some philosophers, if God did do so, we would no longer be responsible or free in what we do. However, it could be that the human will of Christ was created to be so overridden that when the divine nature of Christ "controls" the human nature, there is no coercion or force—the two were meant to work in tandem.

But what does it mean to say that a will is created to be overridden? And if such a will is, in this important way, different from human wills, then it appears that Christ did not genuinely have a human will (which are such that they cannot be so overridden without being undermined); and thereby Christ did not have a genuine human nature. So we think that the two-minds view needs to say much more in defense of the view to ensure the unity of the divine mind and the human mind so as to count as one person.

A more serious concern with the two-minds view is to explain how a single person can have two distinct minds. When we were talking about a human mind and a divine mind, it seems like we were talking about two persons, one person knowing who touched him, and another person not knowing that; and if there are two persons, the view has fallen into the Nestorian heresy.

As a response to this concern, conceptual resources from modern psychology have been employed to explain how a single person might be able to have two (or more) minds. First, consider cases of dissociative identity disorder (formerly known as multiple personality disorder). In some severe cases, one personality will know and desire things that another personality will not know and not desire. Think of the fictional case of Dr. Jekyll and Mr. Hyde. Hyde can keep secrets from Jekyll, and Jekyll can try to frustrate the goals of Hyde. We might even imagine a scenario where Jekyll knows everything that Hyde does and remembers all of Hyde's actions, but Hyde does not know what Jekyll does and does not remember any of Jekyll's actions. Some may regard such an example as a possible case of having a single person with multiple minds.

Another example offered by proponents of a two-minds view comes from split-brain cases. The largest part of the brain (the cerebrum) that is associated with higher functioning, such as consciousness, is made up of two hemispheres that are connected by the corpus callosum, which is a bundle of fibers between both hemispheres. In the past, some doctors used to treat severe forms of epilepsy by cutting the corpus callosum. When they did, strange results occurred. Neuroscientists have claimed that the different hemispheres are in charge of different cognitive and physiological functions. But what some split-brain patients appeared to exhibit was a duality of minds. For example, the left hemisphere is often associated with the physiological functions of the right side of the body, and the right hemisphere is often associated with physiological functions of the left side of the body. Moreover, one hemisphere is usually considered as the one in control of vocal speech. When testing some split-brain patients, doctors would place an object, such as a pipe, on one side of the room. They would then ask the patient what they saw. In some cases, a patient would write down "pipe" while simultaneously speaking and saying that they do not see anything. Many other bizarre occurrences like this seem to indicate that in split-brain cases, we have a divided mind, even though there is a single individual.

One other way of trying to make sense of how a single person can have two minds is to think of the different conscious perspectives one can have in dreams. Sometimes someone can dream as a character in the action, but it seems, as reported by a few people, that they are also conscious of the fact that it is a dream and that they have an overall perspective of what is going on in the dream while simultaneously having the perspective of the character in the action. Thus, there is the conscious perspective of being a character in the dream as well as the *meta-* (or "big picture") perspective. If people are accurately reporting what is going on, then it seems that a single person may have multiple conscious perspectives.

Of course one might be concerned that these cases are abnormal or count as psychological defects, and so some may think that we should not model the incarnation on such bizarre and defective examples. However, defenders of the two-minds view often insist that these cases are being used merely as examples to help explain how it is possible for one person to have multiple minds; it is not to imply that there is anything psychologically defective in the incarnation.

Although the two-minds view has some promise as a viable position, several concerns remain. For example, some argue that there is no conceptual difference between a person and a mind, and so to posit two minds is to posit two persons; but it would be heretical to say that in Jesus there are two persons. However, defenders of the two-minds view have argued that conceptually we can distinguish between being a person and having a mind. Even more fine-grained distinctions have been made, and productive discussion requires deeper inquiry into the cognitive psychology and functioning of human beings. So a lot more philosophical and psychological work needs to be done to make sense of what exactly is going on in cases of multiple minds.

The views discussed at this point have been held by Christian thinkers in the past, especially during the medieval period. However, some models of Christology are relatively new in theological thought. This does not mean we should thereby discount them. After all, a good theory is one that fits well with the teachings of Scripture and coheres with the creedal formulations. Moreover, a plausible theory should avoid logical contradiction while being comprehensible enough, even if it does not completely dispel the mystery (and we wouldn't expect any account to do so). In the next few sections, we will examine and assess some of these more recent proposals.

Relative Identity

One such proposal employs one of the strategies we discussed in the previous chapter on the Trinity, which makes use of the notion of relative identity. Recall that it is typical to treat identity as absolute— that is, identity is a relation that is the same no matter what kind of thing you are talking about. Socrates is identical to Socrates. This chair is identical to this chair. However, some think that identity is not absolute but rather is relative to what kind or sort of thing is being discussed. Remember our earlier example of a clay statue, which on Tuesday is a statue but on Wednesday is flattened by a steamroller. Now we might ask if the object on Tuesday is the same as the object on Wednesday. But the philosopher who uses relative identity might think that the question is ambiguous. The same *what*? Are they the same statue? The answer would be no, since the thing on Wednesday is no longer a statue (after all, if the sculptor walked in the room, she might shout, "You destroyed my statue!"). But are they the same lump of clay? The answer seems to be yes, since lumps of clay can survive a change in shape. So the two objects are the same lump of clay but not the same statue.

As with the doctrine of the Trinity, it is apparent how relative identity can be employed in service of making sense of the doctrine of the incarnation. God the Son is omniscient, but Jesus of Nazareth is limited in knowledge and so is not omniscient. By absolute identity, we would have to say that God the Son is identical to Jesus of Nazareth, and so he is omniscient and not omniscient, which results in the contradiction. However, by using relative identity, we can say that God the Son is not the *same being* as Jesus of Nazareth, but God the Son is the *same person* as Jesus of Nazareth. This seems to avoid the contradiction because God the Son is omniscient and Jesus of Nazareth is not omniscient, and they are not the same being. The relative identity approach, then, can claim that the incarnation involves a single person since God the Son and Jesus of Nazareth are the same person.

Many philosophical theologians do worry about this approach, and usually it is because they have reservations about the idea of relative identity and whether any good sense could be made of it. Moreover, some have worried that the only place that relative identity appears to be applicable is when talking about the Christian God (in the Trinity or incarnation), and so employment of relative identity is an *ad hoc* strategy, which means that there is no good independent reason to use relative identity except to avoid the logical problems of the Trinity and the incarnation. Of course, not all philosophers agree, and a few have made use of relative identity in other areas in metaphysics. Finally, some are concerned that unlike the previous theories, it only provides a linguistic solution—it tells us what we can and cannot say about the incarnation, but many philosophical theologians think that it would be better to give a theory that tells us more about how the incarnation might work (for example, the multiple-parts view and the two-minds view are not merely linguistic solutions).

Kenoticism

We will consider another view that was developed fairly recently in the history of theological thought and has garnered a lot of attention and support, especially within Reformed circles. In the nineteenth century, certain theologians affirmed that Jesus Christ could not be both omniscient and not omniscient. They believed that God divested himself of certain attributes in order to become a human being, a view that is now known as *kenotic* Christology. This view often takes Philippians 2:5–11 as its primary inspiration, where it states that Christ "made himself nothing"—or more literally, "emptied himself"—and the Greek word used there is *hekeinosein*, where the root *kenosis* means "emptying."

Originally, kenotic theorists thought that Christ gave up his divinity or his essential divine attributes, so that it is not true that Christ is still God. So early kenoticists rejected (1) from our discussion above regarding the fundamental problem of Christology. But clearly this contradicts the traditional creeds and arguably even scriptural teaching.

However, recent kenotic theorists (of which one of us is a proponent) maintain that Christ is divine, and so these philosophical theologians have instead claimed that Christ gave up certain divine attributes, but they believe that these attributes that were given up are not *essential* for divinity (that means these attributes could be given up by God while remaining divine). So kenoticism claims that God the Son emptied himself of those properties that are not compatible with his being human or with the way Jesus is depicted in the New Testament Gospels, and so God the Son divested himself of the attributes of omnipotence, omniscience, incorporeality, and so forth in order to become human. Thus, recent kenotic theorists have denied (3) instead of (1), claiming that a divine being need not be omniscient, omnipotent, and so forth.

To remain orthodox, Christ still needs to have the divine attributes that are essential to being God, but what would those be if not omnipotence and omniscience? What has been proposed is that Jesus does have essential divine properties, but that they turn out to be much more complex than we previously thought. Instead of regarding omniscience as essential to being divine, what is essential to being divine is the attribute of being *omniscient unless freely and temporarily choosing to be otherwise.* And the same goes for some of the other divine attributes. Notice that such a property is to be understood as a disjunction (that is, an "either . . . or . . ." statement). So the property claims that a divine being is either omniscient or has freely chosen to temporarily give up the property. So the preincarnate Christ has that disjunctive property while he is omniscient, but he also has that disjunctive property when he freely gives up omniscience. And since Christ had all the attributes essential for being human, he is also human.

There is an obvious concern over the naturalness of such a property. And why would we even want to attribute such a complex property to God? The answer, so say many kenotic theorists, is that we learn about God through Jesus. And so we can learn about the nature of a divine being through what we learn about Christ in Scripture. Jesus appears not to be omniscient in the incarnation while remaining fully divine. So kenotic theorists posit this disjunctive attribute (omniscient unless freely and temporarily choosing to be otherwise) in order to make sense of the biblical data, such as Christ's appearance of being limited in knowledge and limited in power.

Kenotic Christology has many adherents among theologians and philosophers today, but a few concerns linger. One of the central concerns is that it appears to require abandoning what is often known as "perfect-being theology." God is often thought of as the *greatest conceivable being* (which is a view of God that receives its most systematic treatment in the works of Anselm, an eleventh-century philosophical theologian). For any attribute that it is better to have than not to have, God should be thought of as having it (or to be more precise, God has all the "great-making properties" that, taken together, are possible for him to have). However, it seems from perfect-being theology that God should be thought of as being essentially omniscient and essentially omnipotent. So the kenotic approach appears to require rejecting perfect-being theology, but that seems to some theologians to be too high a price to pay.

We think kenotic theorists have responses that can be given to address this concern. One way would be to reject perfect-being theology—perhaps that it is a cost, but maybe not a significant one, especially for someone who thinks that Scripture does not require perfect-being theology. However, we are sympathetic to perfect-being theology, and so we would not want to take this route. So here are two other options. One would be to reassess what it means for a being to be perfect, and which attributes of perfection are more fundamental than others. For example, one might think that having a free range of options matters significantly for a powerful being. However, a perfectly good being will have, in some sense, a constrained range of options since such a being will never be able to do anything bad or wicked. Hence, omnipotence will have to be understood in light of moral goodness; and this can yield an account of power such that sinning or performing morally wrong actions turns out not to be a power but a weakness.

Similarly, one can argue that choosing to divest oneself of nonessential though commonly possessed divine attributes makes for a more perfect being since it gives such a being a kind of freedom that a being who could not divest such attributes would lack. Accordingly, possession of the disjunctive divine properties can fit with a perfect-being theology.

One more proposal, recently advanced by one of us, is to take a Thomistic approach to essential properties. According to one commentator on Aquinas, essential properties are not to be understood in terms of possible worlds (that is, something has an essential property just in case it has that property in all of the possible worlds in which that thing exists), but rather essential properties are to be understood in terms of being disposed to having such a trait.[7] According to this interpretation, Aquinas believed human persons are essentially human (which for Aquinas implied having matter). However, Aquinas also seemed to believe that our souls can and will exist apart from matter after death and before the resurrection. This interpretation claims that we will survive without matter, and yet we will remain essentially human since we will be disposed to being united to matter. So, according to this view, something can have some property essentially while not currently being in possession of that property as long as one is disposed to manifesting that property. It should be clear how this can apply to kenotic Christology. If Christ is disposed to being omnipotent and omniscient, then Christ is essentially omnipotent and essentially omniscient, and this is so even if Christ temporarily divests himself of omnipotence and omniscience. So with this Thomistically inspired theory of essential properties, the kenotic theorist can at least maintain the standard claim in perfect-being theology that divine persons are essentially omnipotent and essentially omniscient.

Another question for kenotic Christology is to ask what happens during Christ's ascension and glorification. Does Christ stay limited in knowledge and power forever, or does he reacquire the attributes of

---

7. For more on this, see Jeffrey Brower, *Aquinas's Ontology of the Material World: Change, Hylomorphism, and Material Objects* (Oxford: Oxford University Press, 2014), 299–300.

omniscience and omnipotence? Some proponents of kenoticism claim that Christ will forever be in a kenotic state; that he never reacquires the properties of omnipotence and omniscience.[8] However, we think theologically there are better reasons to suppose that Christ regains omniscience and omnipotence at his glorification. Traditional Christian belief maintains that Jesus Christ is still human and will be forever. So if the *kenosis* is temporary, then Christ in his glorification will be both omniscient and human. Kenotic theorists must therefore answer the incoherence charge without appeal to *kenosis*—that is, they will have to use another strategy when dealing with the threat of contradiction to account for Christ's state at glorification. Some kenotic theorists agree and so rely on one of the earlier strategies to make sense of Christ's glorified state, and one of us thinks that the qua approach that operates on the subject (i.e., Christ-qua-divinity and Christ-qua-humanity) can be paired with kenoticism to avoid the threat of incoherence. This doesn't seem too problematic, especially since one does not have to hold that a certain approach must handle every threat of incoherence—perhaps one approach handles some cases and another view handles others. So it seems acceptable to us to combine some of the approaches in order to solve the fundamental problem of Christology. This seems to be especially true for kenoticism, because some divine attributes appear to be "un-give-up-able"—attributes such as being necessary, being self-existent, and the like.

Both Attributes

Before we conclude, it is worth mentioning a few approaches that are willing to assert that Christ is both omniscient and not omniscient. That is, on the basis of (1)–(4), they conclude that Christ has both attributes. As we have so far discussed, most theories have tried to avoid making that commitment or have qualified such claims in certain ways—using "qua" operators, showing that these attributes belong

---

8. C. Stephen Evans, "The Self-Emptying of Love: Some Thoughts on Kenotic Christology," in *The Incarnation*, ed. Stephen T. Davis, Daniel Kendall, SJ, and Gerald O'Collins, SJ (Oxford: Oxford University Press, 2002).

to different parts of Christ or to the different minds of Christ, or suggesting that one of these attributes is given up. However, some philosophical theologians think that it is possible for Christians to claim coherently that Christ has both attributes (omniscience and limitation of knowledge) without qualification.

One approach desires to do so by trying to understand the spirit or intention behind the early creedal formulations. Clearly the early Christian thinkers, when trying to articulate the doctrine of the incarnation in the ecumenical creeds, understood that contradictions are logically problematic, and yet they maintained that Christ is omniscient and not omniscient—and they seemed to say so without any qualification. According to a recent philosophical theologian, once we understand the proper way of interpreting these attributions (i.e., once we explicitly spell out the truth conditions for such predications), contradiction can be avoided.[9] When we assert that "Christ is omniscient," what makes that true is that Christ has a nature that is omniscient; and when we claim that "Christ is limited in knowledge," what makes that true is that Christ has a nature that is limited in knowledge. What is unique about this approach is that both statements are indeed true, and hence claiming that Christ is omniscient and not omniscient turns out not to involve a contradiction after all.

Some, however, worry that this view isn't sufficiently different from qua approaches, though superficially it may appear to be so since qua approaches require qualifying the attribution whereas this approach does not. Another serious concern is that this theory does not tell us enough about how it is that Christ can even have more than one nature (we can use language such as "assuming" or "joining," but this obviously needs to be unpacked). This approach would make sense if it were combined with the multiple-parts approach or the multiple-minds approach. But if one wants to avoid such views, then does this approach merely provide a linguistic way out, similar to the relative identity theory of the incarnation?

---

9. Timothy Pawl, *In Defense of Conciliar Christology: A Philosophical Essay* (Oxford: Oxford University Press, 2016).

Finally, we will consider a theory of the incarnation that stands in contrast to all the other views because it insists that claiming that Christ is omniscient and not omniscient is contradictory—and yet some contradictions can turn out true! Before dismissing philosophers as having gone crazy, note that contradictions are necessarily false in what we can call "classical" logic. Logic is merely a system that attempts to map proper reasoning; however, all logical systems have certain limitations in what logic can do and in what it can represent. Because of this, some logicians believe that classical logic is not the correct system to model human reasoning, and there are other "subclassical" forms of logic that have been advanced and worked out—some of which can be extremely difficult for nonlogicians to grasp (such as paraconsistent logic). Moreover, some logical systems allow for more than two truth values (that is, more than just *true* and *false*). Without getting into the details, some recent philosophical theologians think that there are logical systems that allow for some true contradictions, and if philosophical theologians use that to make sense of the incarnation (and the Trinity), then such thinkers can allow that the incarnation (or the Trinity) does contain a contradiction—but in this case, it is a true and acceptable contradiction![10]

We adhere to classical logic (or something like it) as the best system to use when reasoning, and so we are not swayed by these approaches to Christology that permit true contradictions. We only note that such approaches should not be so quickly dismissed, and that the logic worked out in these approaches is sophisticated and worthy of serious consideration.

CONCLUDING THOUGHTS

There are many other philosophical and theological issues related to the incarnation that we did not address. Could Christ have sinned?

---

10. For more on this approach, see Jc Beall, "Christ—a Contradiction," *Journal of Analytic Theology* (2019): 400–33.

Is it impossible for Christ to have sinned? Did Christ have morally significant free will, and how could he be free if he could not have sinned or performed any morally wrong action? Could God the Son become incarnate more than once? Could he have become incarnate more than once at the same time? Could the Father and the Holy Spirit become incarnate? Could all three divine persons become incarnate in the same human being? These questions have been asked and addressed by philosophical theologians, and they are of considerable interest. However, we focused on the logical coherence of claiming that a single person can have two distinct natures, especially since that has been the main focus by philosophical theologians. But we also believe that thinking hard about this issue has apologetic merit, as it can help show that Christians have thought hard about these issues and are not committed to anything logically dubious.

What the preceding chapter and this chapter show is that Christians do not think the doctrine of the Trinity and the doctrine of the incarnation are logically incoherent. The Bible and the early creeds do not tell us exactly how there can be one God in three persons or how one person can have two natures. Hence, Christian thinkers throughout church history and today have tried to make sense of these doctrines by employing philosophical tools and concepts. These tools and concepts are not infallible and are not authoritative, and therefore none of the views discussed in these chapters need to be accepted by all Christians. However, Christians should provide a way of offering a coherent account of these doctrines, especially if they are to answer the charge of believing something illogical or nonsensical. Again, the goal of Christian thinkers is not necessarily to prove these doctrines—most Christians believe them because they have been specially revealed to us by God. Nevertheless, we have a faith that seeks understanding of what we believe.

We hope that as you wrestle with and reflect on these issues, you will seek to avoid false or incoherent views, especially in sermons and studies. This is not merely an academic interest, since all Christians interact with and reflect on the triune God and the incarnate Christ.

Experts in different areas should contribute with their areas of specialty. Biblical theologians should ensure that reflections on these doctrines remain faithful to the witness of Scripture. Systematic theologians can examine the way these doctrines fit with other theological claims. Historical theologians can help with understanding the creedal or doctrinal claims, especially within their historical context—especially since anachronistic interpretations are a common mistake. And philosophical theologians can bring in philosophical concepts and tools to help ensure that what one believes is not logically inconsistent or complete nonsense—the goal is to expound a belief in a doctrine that is logically consistent and intelligible while being faithful to the revelation found in Scripture and the creeds.

We think this is especially true for the church, for we believe these doctrines are not merely for theorizing but for the edification of the church. Church leaders and Christian scholars need to continue to dialogue and work together in offering teaching for the church that comports with the revelation of God and makes an impact in the practical life of the church. Although these topics do not have obvious or immediate practical application, the history of Christian thought shows the importance of doctrinal soundness. Moreover, the church must also be able to defend what Christians believe, especially from objections and criticisms. This requires some basic study of logic, philosophy, theology, church history, and so on, and thus the task of understanding Christian doctrine is the task of the whole church!

FURTHER READINGS

Discussion of some of these themes can be found in chapter 8 ("Was Jesus Mad, Bad, or God?") and chapter 9 ("Is Kenotic Christology Orthodox?") in Stephen T. Davis, *Christian Philosophical Theology* (Oxford: Oxford University Press, 2006). For a great collection of philosophical papers on the incarnation, see Anna Marmodoro and

Jonathan Hill, *The Metaphysics of the Incarnation* (Oxford: Oxford University Press, 2011).

For a discussion of the initial medieval approaches, two seminal (but very advanced) books are Marilyn McCord Adams, *Christ and Horrors: The Coherence of Christology* (Cambridge: Cambridge University Press, 2006); and Richard Cross, *The Metaphysics of the Incarnation: Thomas Aquinas to Duns Scotus* (Oxford: Oxford University Press, 2002). For the "parts" approach, see Eleonore Stump, "Aquinas' Metaphysics of the Incarnation," in her book *Aquinas* (New York: Routledge, 2003); and Brian Leftow, "A Timeless God Incarnate," in *The Incarnation*, ed. Stephen T. Davis, Daniel Kendall, SJ, and Gerald O'Collins, SJ (Oxford: Oxford University Press, 2002). Other chapters in this last book are also quite good in expounding the historical, theological, and philosophical issues pertaining to the incarnation. The classic text for the two-minds view is Thomas Morris, *The Logic of God Incarnate* (Ithaca, NY: Cornell University Press, 1986). For the relative identity approach, see Peter van Inwagen, "Not by Confusion of Substance, but by Unity of Person," in Van Inwagen, *God, Knowledge, and Mystery: Essays in Philosophical Theology* (Ithaca, NY: Cornell University Press, 1995). For kenotic Christology, see Stephen T. Davis, "Is Kenosis Orthodox?" and C. Stephen Evans, "The Self-Emptying of Love: Some Thoughts on Kenotic Christology" in *The Incarnation*, ed. Davis, Kendall, and O'Collins, cited above. For the kenotic strategy of employing the Thomistically inspired approach to essential properties, see Eric T. Yang, "Kenoticism and Essential Divine Properties," *Religious Studies* (forthcoming).

For an influential approach that allows for both attributes to be predicated of Christ, see Timothy Pawl, *In Defense of Conciliar Christology* (Oxford: Oxford University Press, 2016). This book contains a rich study of the history and metaphysics of the doctrine. For the approach that allows for some true contradictions by employing subclassical logic, see Jc Beall, "Christ—A Contradiction." *Journal of Analytic Theology* 7 (2019): 400–33.

REDEMPTION AND ATONEMENT

The Bible is clear that human beings are spiritually lost. There is a huge moral gap between what God expects of us and what we are able to deliver. What God requires is that we love the Lord our God with all our hearts, souls, minds, and strength, and love our neighbors as ourselves (Mark 12:30–31). More broadly, our behavior is to be guided by Scripture. That is, God wants us to be righteous, as he declares: "I am the LORD your God; consecrate yourselves and be holy, because I am holy" (Lev. 11:44). Instead, we are disobedient, rebellious, and prone to lust and violence. Theologians use the word *sin* to cover this fact; sin is essentially not an act but a state of being—a state of separation from God brought about by our failure to obey God's commands. Our actions betray our pride and self-centeredness. We want to run our own lives.

The fact is that we are completely unable to correct this situation; we are unable to save ourselves. No matter how hard we try to be obedient and moral people, we fail miserably every time. Thus, Paul wrote, "For all have sinned and fall short of the glory of God" (Rom. 3:23). So all of us are sinners. That does not mean, of course, that we are all moral monsters like Hitler and Stalin. Human beings are certainly able on occasion to do the morally correct thing. Some people live fairly good moral lives. But the crucial point is that none of the good we do is sufficient to earn divine forgiveness or acceptance, and nothing we do can reconcile us to God from our estrangement from him because of our sin.

But here is a question you might be asking yourself right now: *Why this big emphasis on sin?* I think most people are prepared to admit that they have made mistakes in the moral realm, but most also seem to believe that they are reasonably good persons. Why then do Christians claim that we are all sinners?

Here is a thought experiment. Suppose you could pick anyone you wanted to follow you around for six months. Suppose you picked your grandmother, who loves you and is thoroughly honest. Her job would be to record any moral judgment you made during that period, statements like, "It's wrong to lie to your boss" or "Visiting your sick friend was a good thing to do" or "It's wrong to pollute the atmosphere." At the end of the six months, your grandmother would be asked to collect all the moral judgments you've expressed and to collate them into a list of judgments that we might call your "moral code" (and if it didn't capture the entire moral code, it would at least constitute much of it).

Next your grandmother would be asked to follow you around for another six months. This time she would record not what you say but what you do. She would note whether you consistently follow your own moral rules. Now, if you are like the two of us, and indeed like most people, there would be a discontinuity between your moral judgments and at least some of your moral actions. Christians mean something like this when they charge people with being sinners. We humans do not do very well at living up even to our own moral standards, let alone the undoubtedly much stricter standards that we find in the Ten Commandments and the teachings of Jesus. A large moral gap exists between what we should be and what we in fact are.

The Bible is clear that our redemption from sin occurs not because of anything we do but because of the work of Christ, especially the death of Christ on the cross. And it occurs not because we earn it; it is a free gift of God. This is called *grace*.

But precisely *how* is our redemption accomplished? *Atonement* is a word in theology that refers to the means or mechanism of our redemption. The core idea is located even in the etymology of the word: *at-one-ment*—which is our being made one with or reconciled to God. A theory of atonement tries to explain how the incarnation, the teachings, and especially the death and resurrection of Christ brought such reconciliation about. There are many atonement themes in the Bible, but Scripture does not provide us with any full-blown theory of atonement. And unlike the doctrines of the Trinity and the incarnation, there were no early creedal or conciliar pronouncements that clearly delineated the boundaries for an acceptable account of the atonement. Accordingly, Christian theologians throughout history have offered several different theories of the atonement, all of them based on various scriptural texts or themes. They can be classified in different ways, and we will discuss several proposals in this chapter. We will find that there is some truth in all the theories, as well as some significant deficiencies.

But before proceeding to those theories, we can ask some other questions: Was the atoning work of Christ necessary? Christians have disagreed over this question. Some think that it was absolutely necessary that Christ die so that we might be reconciled to God. That is, there was no other way for the atonement to be accomplished but through Christ's death. Historically, it was much more widely held that Christ's atoning work was not absolutely necessary—that God could have reconciled human creatures to himself through some other means. Some have instead asserted that the atonement was only conditionally necessary, though saying this is ambiguous. Does it mean that necessarily, if human beings are to be reconciled to God, then Christ had to die? Or does it mean that Christ's death is a necessary condition, that if Christ did not die on the cross, then we are not reconciled to God? It seems to us that philosophers and theologians sometimes mean different things in their claim that Christ's death was conditionally necessary. Furthermore, some aver that it was not necessary at all that Christ die for our sins but that it was fitting or appropriate that he do so. That is, even if Christ could have reconciled us to God through other means, it in some way makes the most sense given God's nature, human nature, and the wreckage of our sin that Christ die on the cross. Hence, Christians can disagree on whether the atoning work was necessary (and what it even means for it to be necessary).

Another question often asked is this: If God is a God of love, why doesn't God just forgive those who are truly repentant? Why did Christ have to die on the cross? Of course, we Christians do hold that God is infinitely loving and will forgive those who truly repent. But it is easy to underestimate the seriousness of sin. The separation of human beings from God, and the resultant depths of human depravity, is the worst thing that has happened in human history. Think of all the cruelty, pain, and suffering that human beings have heaped on each other. Think of the African slave trade. Think of the Holocaust of World War II. Those are not the sorts of events about which God can say to their perpetrators, "It's okay; just forget about it." It is not good or appropriate for forgiveness to be granted lightly. Doing so trivializes sin, the sinner, and the victims or offended party. Something radical had to be done to change the whole moral situation. Since that "something" cannot be achieved by human beings acting on their own, it had to be brought about by God. And that "something" is what we are talking about in this chapter: atonement. The deep connection between atonement and the cross (as well as the Old Testament sacrificial system) is probably why the author to the Hebrews wrote, "Without the shedding of blood there is no forgiveness" (Heb. 9:22).

So, given that it was either necessary or fitting that Christ atone for our sins, how exactly could it be accomplished? Philosophers and theologians have devised several theories, each of which tries to capture some biblical text or metaphor. The views that we explain below are not exhaustive of all the options, but they provide a decent sample of the kind of work that philosophical theologians have brought to bear on this issue.

RANSOM THEORY

The first, and perhaps oldest, view is the *ransom theory*. Although we find a variety of atonement themes among the church fathers, this was probably the dominant theme of atonement in the early church. We can find suggestions of it in the work of church fathers such as Irenaeus, Origen, and Augustine. To be sure, claiming that any church father had a *theory* of atonement, a systematic treatment worthy of the name *theory*, is difficult. That said, discussion of atonement was central in their thinking, and it is clear that the theme of ransom was prominent, though there are disputes about this with regard to what these historical figures actually believed.

The central idea of the ransom theory is that, because of our sinfulness, we human beings are in the clutches of the devil; we are all, so to speak, his prisoners. And a ransom had to be paid for us to be set free from that bondage. Proponents of the ransom theory often cite Mark 10:45, where Jesus said, "For even the Son of Man did not come to be served, but to serve, and to give his life as a ransom for many." And Paul wrote to the Christians in Corinth, "You were bought at a price" (1 Cor. 6:20). In some admittedly crude versions of the theory, God tricked the devil: he offered Jesus's death on the cross as a kind of bait to Satan. When Jesus died, the devil did allow us to go free, but God then fooled the devil by raising Jesus from the dead. Something similar to this theory is found in C. S. Lewis's *The Lion, the Witch and the Wardrobe*, though Lewis probably did not intend for that story to provide his particularly favored theory of the atonement.[1]

The strong point of this theory is that we human beings are indeed enslaved to sin and are unable to free ourselves. Moreover, it seems true that a price had to be paid. As we noted above, because of his holiness and justice, God could not just say about our disobedience, "It's no big thing; don't worry about it."

However, we find some concerns with this theory. One problem is that it makes it sound as if God and the devil are like sovereign rulers who must negotiate with each other as equals. But, in fact, the devil is a fallen creation of God to whom God owes nothing. God and the

---

1. C. S. Lewis. *The Lion, The Witch and the Wardrobe* (London: Geoffrey Bles, 1950).

devil are not in competition with each other—God's power is so much greater. Additionally, God is not usually depicted as the rival of the devil; rather, the devil is usually represented as being pitted against an angel, such as Michael (Rev. 12:7).

Moreover, the cruder version of the theory makes it sound as if God is being deceitful by tricking the devil, and it is hard to square God's "bait and switch" with the claim that God is morally perfect or with the biblical passages that assert that God cannot lie (Titus 1:2; Heb. 6:18). And even if positing deceit in God can be avoided, doesn't our salvation amount to much more than defeating the devil? Even if human beings are no longer in the clutches of the devil, no mention is made regarding our situation of being in sin and hence guilty before God. Yes, we are rescued, but we are still guilty, and the ransom theory, at least in its cruder version, does not appear to take that fact into account.

In recent times, a variant of the ransom theory has been developed that focuses not only on victory over the devil but also on victory over sin and death. This view has been called the *Christus Victor*[2] theory (which means in Latin "Christ the Victor"), and was championed by twentieth-century Swedish theologian Gustav Aulen.[3] Under this account, Christ's life, death, and resurrection decisively defeated evil, death, and all the forces that oppose God's rule. The outcome of the cosmic struggle between good and evil was decisively settled in Christ. Of course, evil still exists, but its fate is sealed. To make this clearer, consider the following analogy: once the Allies had achieved a successful lodgment in Normandy in June 1944, it was evident that Germany would be defeated. The Nazis fought on for about nine more months, and many more people on both sides were killed, but the Nazis' cause was hopeless. Since God has once and for all defeated evil and death, human beings (who were once enslaved to sin) can be saved. Thus, Paul wrote, "In Christ all will be made alive. . . . 'Where, O death, is your victory?

---

2. Sometimes in the theological literature, the ransom theory and Christus Victor are regarded as the same view.

3. Gustaf Aulen, *Christus Victor*, trans. H. G. Herbert (New York: Macmillan, 1969).

Where, O death, is your sting?'" (1 Cor. 15:22, 55). So while sin remains, evil has been vanquished because of Christ's actions in the world.

This theory, too, looks to be correct in what it claims, but it has also been criticized for being an incomplete account of atonement. For example, some are concerned that it fails to include the role of a human response of faith. Moreover, the ransom theory says very little about exactly how the human condition is remedied—how is it that our sins have been forgiven or that we have been reconciled to God? Perhaps more importantly, the ransom theory does not appear by itself to capture all of what Scripture says about the atonement. Hence, it is far too incomplete to count as an adequate theory of the atonement.

MORAL INFLUENCE THEORY

We will next consider the moral influence theory, which was developed by the early medieval theologian Peter Abelard (1079–1142), and such a theory appears to enjoy some popularity today, especially in liberal Protestantism. According to the moral influence theory, Christ's death on the cross was the result of his perfect obedience, and Jesus's life and death are for us an inspiring and transformative example of the obedience to God that we human beings should practice. When we seriously contemplate Jesus's passion and death, it breaks our hearts and inspires us to live a similar life. The cross shows us the depths of God's love for us and stimulates our love for God. We then want to emulate Jesus's life by being obedient to God. The essence of the atonement, then, is the influence it has on us, where Jesus serves as the perfect model that we should strive to imitate.

One passage of Scripture that highlights this aspect of the atonement is in 1 John 4:9: "This is how God showed his love among us: He sent his one and only Son into the world that we might live through him." Christ's life, as well as his death, manifests the divine love, and so Christ is an exemplar for his disciples. Moreover, several passages in Scripture focus on imitating Christ. For example, Paul states that we should imitate him just as he imitates Christ (1 Cor. 11:1). And in Matthew 11:29–30, we are told by Christ to take his yoke and to learn from him. But a yoke is what farmers would put on an ox to be used in farming. Often a younger ox would be hitched to the same yoke as an ox that had already been out in the field, and the younger ox would eventually follow the gait of the older ox, thereby making the task of plowing the field easier. Similarly, we are exhorted to imitate the manner of Christ's life, thereby making the task of life easy, for his "burden is light." So the imitation theme already runs throughout the New Testament (and even the Old Testament, as we are to be holy just as God is holy). So Christ serves as the perfect exemplar for his followers.

Some philosophical theologians worry that this theory is problematic if Christ's life and death serve merely as an inspiring moral example. For example, some are concerned that there is no reason why Jesus had to suffer and die a horrific death on the cross if the only purpose was to serve as a moral example for us. Moreover, there does not seem to be any *atoning* taking place in Christ's death, especially if it is merely an example of self-sacrificial love.

However, some recent philosophers argue that Abelard's actual view does not regard Christ's actions as a mere moral example.[4] Some philosophers think that there is an element of penal substitution (which we discuss below) in Abelard's theory. However, it also appears that Abelard highlights Christ's love as a *transforming* agent so that it can free people from their enslavement to sin. Accordingly, we can receive the grace of God and be free to do what is right and good through Christ's death. If we cooperate with it, the divine love revealed in Christ's passion and death has the power to transform us.

The more nuanced and sophisticated version of the moral influence theory is powerful: to consider seriously the death of Christ on our

---

4. Philip Quinn, "Abelard on Atonement: 'Nothing Unintelligible, Arbitrary, Illogical, or Immoral About it,'" in *Reasoned Faith*, ed. Eleonore Stump (Ithaca, NY: Cornell University Press, 1993).

behalf does indeed break the hearts of many people and make them want to change their lives. As far as it goes, the moral influence theory seems to be true.

But does it go far enough? We think that it does not, especially if it amounts to the idea that Christ's life and death mainly serve as an example for us. We can try to change for the better, to turn over a new leaf and live obediently, but for us actually to do so is another matter. It does not seem as if an inspiring moral example is enough to bring that about. Doubtless there have been many noble and inspiring deaths in human history. Consider the trial and death of Socrates as recorded in Plato's dialogues *The Apology* and *The Phaedo*. Was Jesus's death on that same level? We think not. Atonement had to do something more than merely inspire us; it had to do something radical to change the moral situation.

The sophisticated version does claim that Christ's life and death indeed had such a transformative power. However, it is not clear exactly how it can transform us over and above merely inspiring us. Exactly how is transformation supposed to occur? Explanation or elaboration of this aspect would make the theory more plausible since it can show the remedial effect of Christ's atoning work.

Another shortcoming raised against the moral influence theory is that it completely leaves out any notion of divine justice and the satisfaction of such justice. In disobedience, we have failed to give God what we should have given him, and the sophisticated moral influence theory that includes a transforming power does not address this crucial aspect of the atonement and hence offers an incomplete picture of what Christ accomplished in his atoning work.

SATISFACTION: PENAL SUBSTITUTION

As the situation stands today, the most influential approach to the atonement falls under a broad family of views that we can call *satisfaction* theories, which can be traced back to the great medieval philosopher and theologian Anselm of Canterbury (1033–1109). Anselm had a kind of courtroom analogy in mind; he argued that when we sin, we fail to pay God the honor due him or we commit a grave injustice against God. Some who take this approach appear to view God in some ways like a medieval king to whom his subjects rightly owe obedience and deference. But by our disobedience we instead rebel against God's rule. Accordingly, we are guilty. In response to our wrongdoing, God's holy nature requires that there be punishment or adequate compensation. So we owe God a debt that must be satisfied, but the trouble is that we cannot possibly pay it. Thankfully, God pays the debt himself by becoming incarnate and making satisfaction on our behalf.

As stated, the satisfaction for our wrongdoing against God requires either punishment or compensation. For those who focus on punishment, the most popular version is the *penal substitution* theory, whereas those who focus on compensation have developed theories that we can call *penitential substitution* or *penitential satisfaction* theories. Let us first examine penal substitution views.

According to the penal substitution theory, God himself paid the penalty for us, as a gift of love, by the death of his Son on the cross. Thus, Paul wrote, "God demonstrates his own love for us in this: While we were still sinners, Christ died for us" (Rom. 5:8). Isaiah 53 appears to prophesy that Jesus would die in our place. The penalty was incurred against human beings, so justice requires that it had to be paid by a human being; but humans cannot pay the penalty—only God can. Hence, only someone who was both God and man could pay the penalty.

Some questions naturally arise: Was Christ being punished for our sins? Proponents of penal substitution disagree. Some maintain that Christ was being punished, for our sins were placed on Christ, and hence Christ endured the punishment we deserve. Those who take this line claim that it is possible for someone to be punished even if they are not guilty or bear no fault of wrongs committed. So Christ, who had no guilt, could be punished for our sins. However, other penal substitutionary proponents claim that it makes no sense for an innocent person to be justly punished. Hence, many proponents of penal substitution claim that Christ was not being punished. Rather, Christ endured what *would have been punishment* had we had to endure it, but what Christ underwent was not strictly punishment. So our sin was imputed into Christ (and Christ's righteousness was imputed into us), and so Christ was treated as though he were a guilty sinner, even though he was actually blameless and innocent (and we are treated as blameless and innocent even though we are guilty sinners). However, Christ became our substitute and received what would have been our punishment, namely, suffering and ultimately death. Christ thereby served as our representative in his reception of suffering and death, taking for humanity what should have been given to all human beings.

While a popular view, especially among Protestant Christians, some are concerned that penal substitution makes no sense because it requires either punishing an innocent individual or enacting treatment that would count as punishment on that individual, and that would be unjust. We have intuitions that only the guilty should be punished, and the innocent should not receive punishment or should not receive what would have been punishment had it been endured by the guilty party. For example, if a person murdered someone, we would think it unfair that the person's mother was sent to jail, even if the mother was willing to take the place of her son. It is the guilty son who deserves to be in jail, and his failure to be thrown in jail seems to violate the demands of justice. Moreover, justice appears to be violated in throwing the mother into jail because she is innocent. So how can God allow for an innocent victim, namely Christ, to experience the punishment that we, the guilty party, deserve? Some may see this as a double violation of justice because the guilty are not punished and the innocent receives punishment or the treatment that would count as punishment if endured by the guilty.

Interestingly, a very notable atheist argued that our intuitions regarding vicarious punishment are mixed and inconsistent—that we think in some cases it is permissible and in others that it is not. Hence, he thinks that this is not just a problem for proponents of penal substitution but for anyone who thinks hard about the nature of punishment.[5] Philosophers have spent quite some time inquiring into the nature of and justification for punishment, and hence a full evaluation of penal substitution (whether critical or in defense) requires understanding some issues in philosophy of law and competing theories of punishment (for example, retribution, deterrence, etc.). From this approach, some philosophical theologians argue that there are clear cases in which vicarious punishment or vicarious liability does indeed take place, in particular the vicarious liability that employers have for actions performed by their employees.[6] Although an employee may engage in illegal activities, the employer can be penalized for these actions even if the employer did not directly perform any of the illegal actions.

Other critics of penal substitution worry that such a theory does not make room for genuine forgiveness. Forgiving a debt owed amounts to waiving the debt; it involves a declaration that nothing more needs to be paid. So if God forgives human beings for their failure to obey and keep God's commands, then the full enactment of punishment would not be necessary. And yet penal substitution theorists seem to claim that the full enactment of punishment had to be paid by Christ, and hence there was no waiving of punishment, and so there was no forgiveness. Of course, penal substitution theorists have offered responses to this and other concerns, and so discussion of the merits or flaws of penal substitution are rich and worth exploring. And we invite you to think of potential ways of mitigating such concerns or determining whether the penal substitution theory should be abandoned.

---

5. David Lewis, "Do We Believe in Penal Substitution?" *Philosophical Papers* 26, no. 3 (1997): 203–9.

6. For more on this, see William Lane Craig, *The Atonement* (Cambridge: Cambridge University Press, 2018).

SATISFACTION:
PENITENTIAL SUBSTITUTION

Because of some of these concerns, other philosophical theologians have instead focused on *penitential substitution*, with many contemporary philosophers favoring a version that is associated with the medieval theologian and philosopher Thomas Aquinas (1225–74). Similar to the previous theory, Christ serves as a substitute for human sinners. But the focus here is not on punishment but what is owed to God. In fact, the term *satisfaction* etymologically means to "do enough." Some contemporary proponents of penitential substitution think that the real problem that the atonement is supposed to solve has been posed in the wrong kind of way. For example, one way of setting up the problem appears to have a God who is unwilling to be reconciled to human beings until an adequate amount has been paid. However, another way of framing the issue is to see that the problem is not on the part of God but on the part of human beings, in particular that our wills are not in conformity with the will of God. Now Christ offers to God what human beings did not, a perfect life of humility, obedience, and love, which was exhibited most fully in his self-sacrificial death on the cross. So Christ offers himself to God the Father to make up for what was not (but should have been) given to him.

Consider the following example.[7] Suppose that a child is commanded to stay out of his mother's study but disobeys, and while throwing a ball around, he accidentally destroys a precious item that belongs to his mother. Furthermore, suppose that the child does not feel sorry for what he has done. A severance occurs in the relationship between the mother and her child because the child does not properly love the mother in the way he should, by loving and caring

---

7. This example is an adaptation of a case provided in Eleonore Stump, "Atonement according to Aquinas," in *Philosophy and the Christian Faith*, ed. Thomas Morris (Notre Dame, IN: University of Notre Dame Press, 1988).

for the things she cares about. The fault, then, is not with the mother, who may desire to be united to her son, but with the son, who either feels guilt or shame and so may hide away from his mother, or out of maliciousness or a lack of concern doesn't feel those things. Either way, harmony between mother and son is lacking. Now suppose the child has a change of heart and wants to make things right but doesn't know how to do so. Furthermore, imagine that the child has an older sister who recognizes the young child's plight and, at the request of the child, decides to help him. Since she is older, she can sacrifice her time and money to purchase a replacement of the precious item, and they can together return the gift to their mother while the young child offers his sincerest apology. In this way, the older sister makes satisfaction for her younger brother's action. If the young child is truly repentant, he can regain harmony with his mother.

Similarly, human beings can adjoin themselves to Christ and so offer the same gift of Christ as one that they are giving to God. According to this Thomistically inspired view, God does not need anything and has not really lost anything. However, if God desires that our wills be in conformity with his will, then he will receive the gift because it indicates that our wills have returned to conformity with his will since Christ's will is in perfect conformity with the Father's will.

Under another contemporary version of penitential satisfaction, the way to make sense of satisfaction is to think about how human persons can be reconciled to another when they have wronged someone. What appears to be required for reconciliation are four key elements:

(1) apology,
(2) repentance,
(3) reparation,
(4) and penance.[8]

---

8. For more on this account, see Richard Swinburne, *Responsibility and Atonement* (Oxford: Oxford University Press, 1989).

Suppose Bob wronged you by breaking into your home. Bob smashed your window, climbed in, and stole something valuable. Now suppose Bob felt guilty and wanted to make things right again. What would Bob have to do to restore his relationship with you? First, it seems that Bob would have to apologize and repent; that is, Bob would have to show genuine remorse—perhaps come to you and say sincerely, "I am sorry"—and exhibit a change of heart. It also seems that Bob would have to make reparation—he would have to fix the window or pay to have it fixed and would have to return the stolen item or at least pay to replace it (that would be reparation). However, it seems that Bob would also have to give a gift or perform an act of service as a sign of his regret; that is, he would have to do more to acknowledge the seriousness of his wrongdoing and his desire to be reconciled with you. Perhaps he would come back every week to mow your lawn or to drop off a meal (that would be penance). With his apology, repentance, reparation, and penance, the relationship between Bob and you can be restored.

According to this version of penitential satisfaction, the same applies with regard to our offenses against God. We can and must apologize and repent to God for our sins, and this is something that human beings can do. But when it comes to our relationship with God, we cannot offer adequate reparation and penance. We can do nothing to make up for the damages or to pay back what is owed or to give God more in return for the wrong we have committed. But Christ lived a perfect human life and accordingly is capable of doing so. He voluntarily endured a death that he intended as a sacrifice on our behalf. This is sufficient for a merciful God to offer forgiveness to those who identify themselves with Christ, worship God, and plead the atoning death of Christ.

Some philosophers have objected by claiming that it makes no sense to make reparation and penance by offering up someone else's sacrifice, and especially someone else's death. Moreover, some have criticized penitential satisfaction by claiming that God does not require reparation or penance since God does not experience "damages"—nothing is lost or taken from God when we sin. On the second point, defenders of Anselm's theory need not hold that God—like an insulted feudal monarch—was in any way damaged or injured. They instead stress the idea that it would be unjust for God to ignore our sins; the penalty for them must be paid. But the first point is the more serious criticism. In reply to it, defenders of Anselm always stress the voluntary nature of Christ's death—he died for us out of his own free choice.

Satisfaction theories—whether penal or penitential—have had a deep resonance with many Christians. It is undoubtedly correct to say that we are guilty before God, that there are consequences (i.e., sin requires punishment or compensation), and that in dying, Christ paid the penalty or the debt for us. It also underscores the fact that forgiveness is not easy; grace is not cheap. But some philosophers have also criticized this general approach as being too "objective"; that is, the picture seems to entail that God does a certain act and it, all by itself, saves us. But what about the "subjective" requirement of our response of faith? Doesn't our salvation require that too? In this way, the moral influence theory may have some advantage over satisfaction theories. Moreover, some see a slight tension in the view of God in this theory: it looks as if God repays with one part of his nature (the loving part) a debt incurred against another part of his nature (the part involving holiness and justice). And that may seem problematic. The question, then, is whether satisfaction theories can be presented in such a way as to avoid these untoward implications.

DIVINE WRATH

Before closing our discussion, we want to highlight a biblical theme that is pervasive throughout Scripture and yet is often rejected or ignored by philosophical theologians as well as by some church preachers and teachers—the theme of God's wrath. In discussions of atonement,

divine wrath is sometimes mentioned to caricature a view of a vin-
dictive God that must be placated through the suffering and death of
Christ. We, however, think that the caricature can be rejected while
retaining the importance of this biblical theme.

Divine wrath is God's opposition to sin and evil, which seems to
follow from God's morally perfect nature. The psalmist said of God,
"We are consumed by your anger and terrified by your indignation.
You have set our iniquities before you, our secret sins in the light
of your presence" (Ps. 90:7–8). God's wrath is an expression of his
righteous nature, but it is also an expression of his love for human
beings. Suppose a child was engaged in wrong actions by hurting others.
A good parent would naturally be angry with the child, but this anger
would not preclude the parent's love for her child. In fact, the more
a parent loves her child, the likelier she will be angry, for the parent
will be disappointed that the child is not becoming the kind of person
that the child can and should be. Moreover, the parent might also care
for the victim of the child's malfeasance. Of course, real parents often
burst out in anger beyond what is appropriate or out of lack of relevant
information. God, however, is omniscient and so does not make irrational leaps. Moreover, God does not go beyond what is appropriate,
and his anger against human beings is out of his great love for them,
wanting them to become the way they were created to be, as perfect
image bearers of God.

God's wrath, then, is more akin to righteous indignation. The
absence of divine wrath at the pervasive wickedness in our world would
be a defect in God, which is impossible because God is morally perfect.

By incorporating the notion of wrath in a theory of atonement, the
seriousness, gravity, and extent of Christ's atoning work as depicted
in the Scriptures can be better captured. If Christ is trying to destroy
the elements in us that are the cause of our guilt, it is natural that God
would direct his wrath at destroying that element. Moreover, experiencing God's anger would be akin to experiencing God's love, for
God disciplines his children in order that they will become more like

Christ—that their wills will be in conformity to his will. The experience of divine wrath, then, can be a sign of a loving parent who seeks to discipline his children and to restore a relationship. And divine wrath shows that the problem of sin is not a light or small problem. Injustice and disobedience against God is a grave and serious problem, for it yields separation from God. To return to a text already mentioned, given how bad sin is, it makes sense that the author of Hebrews would write that "without the shedding of blood there is no forgiveness" (Heb. 9:22). And hence it is always difficult and costly to rectify a terribly wrong situation.

This truth goes some distance in helping us understand why Christ underwent a horrifying sacrifice. Some theologians think God should have merely waived off our debt and forgiven us without any sacrifice, or at least that God could have done so. But to see what is wrong with that picture, consider ancient tragedies. The phrase *deus ex machina*, which literally means "God out of a machine," referred to the quick and easy solution to a problem in ancient plays. For instance, it was as though Zeus was lowered to the stage by a machine and resolved everything by one swift edict. Early on, people recognized that plays or stories with a *deus ex machina* ending were unrealistic and literarily deficient. We suspect that the reason why humans have ubiquitously found such stories weak is because it takes a great cost to rectify a terrible wrong.

So God's wrath reminds us how great a wrong our sin is and why so much had to be paid to rectify our situation. And as long as we construe God's wrath as coming from a loving parent (and not from a bank collector or an impartial judge in a courtroom), wrath is a corollary of God's great love for us.

Not only does divine wrath explain why such a great sacrifice was needed or appropriate, but it can also be employed to address certain objections to satisfaction theories. We are quite sympathetic with penitential substitution theories, but such theories have been criticized on the basis that God cannot be harmed.[9] But if God cannot be harmed,

---

9. Richard Cross, "Atonement without Satisfaction," *Religious Studies* 37 (2001): 397–416.

then God suffers no loss. So no reparation or penance is necessary—all that is necessary is apology (and perhaps repentance). But human beings can carry out an apology (and repentance) on their own, so the penitential substitution theory appears to be too strong in demanding reparation and penance, which was paid by Christ.

We do think, however, that there is a sense in which God can be harmed. Of course it will not be the kind of biological or even psychological harm that can occur to human beings. But taking the analogy of a parent and a child, a parent can be harmed while perceiving her child harming himself. The child may be engaged in behavior that only directly harms himself, yet we think there is a reasonable sense in which the parent can be harmed as well. Of course this harm does not diminish or undermine any of God's capacities or attributes. But when a parent gets angry at a child, such anger can constitute harm for the parent. Similarly, we think that God may be harmed in a similar way, watching his children directly inflict damages on themselves and one another.

Moreover, utilizing divine wrath can also address this objection by showing that mere apology is not enough. It is not enough for perpetrators just to say, "I'm sorry," as though that would suffice. The grievous wrong they performed requires much more. As we've been reiterating, it takes a great and terrible cost to rectify a wrong. And so we affirm the need for reparation and penance, which is something that we alone cannot give to God but only through what Christ has done on our behalf.

CONCLUDING THOUGHTS

Many different themes and metaphors are brought out in discussion of the atonement: ransom, victory, moral example, penalty, substitution, satisfaction, and so on. We should not think that these theories are exclusive of each other—some might mix or match these views, though which ideas are more fundamental will still be debated. In fact, most of the plausible theories of atonement do take several of these views and combine them for a theory that attempts to avoid several of the objections mentioned as well as capturing more of the ways salvation is described in Scripture. For example, a penal substitutionary theorist might include the idea of ransom or moral example but regard these notions as subservient to the primary notion of penal substitution. And many penitential satisfaction theories also focus on the moral influence of Christ's perfect life and voluntary death. So an adequate theory of the atonement need not focus on a reductionist or isolated approach to the atonement. A pluralist approach seems to be the right way forward. We are sympathetic to such a pluralist approach, though we would argue that penitential substitution would have to play a foundational role in such a theory, even while claiming that Christ's great act of love can transform and inspire us.

As noted, although the Christian church has officially declared how the doctrines of incarnation and Trinity work, it has never officially declared how the atonement works. Accordingly, theologians have felt free to propose various theories, some of which we have just discussed (and there are of course other theories, for example, merit theories and governmental theories). No one theory is theologically mandatory. In a way, this is not surprising. God is mysterious, transcendent, far above us. We are unable to capture fully the depths of God's love for us or the complexities of God's methods of saving us. Moreover, the Bible describes our salvation with many different concepts—reconciliation, forgiveness, justification, redemption, regeneration, propitiation, and others, all with different nuances. It is not easy to combine all these themes into a comprehensive theory. Accordingly, we want to emphasize that Christians are not forced to choose one of the theories. And, in fact, we can gain insights from all of them. Each draws attention to some crucial aspect of what God has done for us.

Reflecting on the atonement should first elicit the response of worship and praise to a God who loved us so much that despite our rebellion he has carried out his plan to reconcile us to himself. However, those of us who embrace the motto "faith seeking understanding" are inclined to understand how it is that God accomplishes this great task. By no means should theorizing get in the way of rejoicing and worshiping our Savior and Redeemer. But theorizing about the atonement can deepen our appreciation of God as we come to grasp to what extent God loves us by atoning for our sins. We can speak from our own personal experience that thinking and theorizing about the atonement has only increased our awe of and gratitude of the God who is for us and loves us.

FURTHER READINGS

For historical treatment of these theories, we recommend reading classical Christian authors, for example, Athanasius, Origen, Gregory of Nyssa, Augustine, Abelard, Anselm, Thomas Aquinas, John Calvin, and many more. For a nice theological overview of some of the theories we discussed in this chapter, see James Beilby and Paul R. Eddy, eds., *The Nature of the Atonement* (Downers Grove, IL: InterVarsity Press, 2006). For helpful discussion of the biblical, historical, theological, and philosophical issues pertaining to atonement and associated themes, see Stephen T. Davis, Daniel Kendall, SJ, and Gerald O'Collins, SJ, eds., *The Redemption* (Oxford: Oxford University Press, 2004).

For discussion of the ransom theory/*Christus Victor*, see Gustaf Aulen, *Christus Victor*, trans. H. G. Herbert (New York: Macmillan, 1969). For contemporary discussion of the moral influence theory, see Philip Quinn's "Abelard on Atonement: 'Nothing Unintelligible, Arbitrary, Illogical, or Immoral about it,'" in Eleonore Stump, ed., *Reasoned Faith* (Ithaca, NY: Cornell University Press, 1993). For a defense of penal substitution theory, see William Lane Craig's chapter "Christian Doctrines III: Atonement," in J. P. Moreland and William Lane Craig, *Philosophical Foundations of a Christian Worldview*

(Downers Grove, IL: InterVarsity Press, 2017). See also Craig, *The Atonement* (Cambridge: Cambridge University Press, 2018). For penitential substitution/satisfaction theories, see Richard Swinburne, *Responsibility and Atonement* (Oxford: Oxford University Press, 1989); Eleonore Stump, "Atonement according to Aquinas," in *Philosophy and the Christian Faith*, ed. Thomas Morris (Notre Dame, IN: University of Notre Dame Press, 1988); and her more recent book, *Atonement* (Oxford: Oxford University Press, 2018).

For more on divine wrath and its relation to atonement, see chapter 12, "The Wrath of God and the Blood of Christ," in Stephen T. Davis, *Christian Philosophical Theology* (Oxford: Oxford University Press, 2006); and Eric T. Yang and Stephen T. Davis, "Atonement and the Wrath of God," in *Locating Atonement: Explorations in Constructive Dogmatics*, ed. Oliver D. Crisp and Fred Sanders (Grand Rapids: Zondervan, 2015).

RESURRECTION AND LIFE AFTER DEATH

What happens to us after we die? Some people believe that our souls will live without bodies forever. Others accept reincarnation, where souls will enter into different bodies throughout many cycles, perhaps until the soul can eventually escape and lose itself into some impersonal reality. In contrast to these, traditional Christianity holds to belief in the resurrection. When Christ returns, our bodies will be raised from the dead. While philosophers have offered arguments for life after death or the immortality of the soul, belief in the resurrection arises entirely from revelation. Christians believe that we will be raised from the dead because of the promises of God and the resurrection of Christ, whose resurrection was the "firstfruits of those who have fallen asleep" (1 Cor. 15:20). All human beings will be resurrected, as we read in Daniel 12:2 that "multitudes who sleep in the dust of the earth will awake: some to everlasting life, others to shame and everlasting contempt," and in John 5:28–29 that "a time is coming when all who are in their graves will hear his voice and come out—those who have done what is good will rise to live, and those who have done what is evil will rise to be condemned."

Traditionally, Christians have believed that the future resurrected person will be identical to the original person, that all persons will be resurrected, and that the resurrection will occur at some future time when Christ returns in glory. However, these traditional claims have been disputed, leading to several theological debates on these matters. For example, some theologians aver that the future resurrected person will not be the original person but a replica. Others claim that only the righteous will be resurrected, perhaps because the wicked will be annihilated and so will not exist forever (we discuss this more in chapter 7). Finally, there is disagreement on the timing of the resurrection, some even claiming that resurrection occurs immediately after death. We will not be discussing these issues here but will instead focus on the question of how resurrection of the same body is even possible.

DUALISM AND MATERIALISM

Before we get into that discussion, we need to cover some preliminary philosophical issues, in particular the nature of human persons. Quite broadly, we can categorize views of human persons as a version of dualism or materialism (although these views are not exhaustive of all the options):

> **DUALISM:** Human persons are identical to immaterial souls (or to a composite of immaterial souls and physical bodies).
> **MATERIALISM:** Human persons are identical to some material object.

Note that materialism does not tell us which material object human persons are identical to, and that is because materialists disagree. Here are some options for materialist views of human persons:

> **ANIMALISM:** Human persons are identical to human animals.
> **BRAINISM (EMBODIED MINDS VIEW):** Human persons are identical to brains (or cerebra).
> **CONSTITUTION VIEW:** Human persons are material things constituted by human animals (but are not identical to human animals).

FOUR-DIMENSIONALISM:[1] Human persons are identical to space-time "worms," objects spread across both space and time.

These are just a sample of some of the main materialist views.

While dualism, or some variation of it, has been the dominant view held by most Christians throughout church history, Christianity is, strictly speaking, compatible with both dualism and materialism. So we need to be careful about the word *materialism*, for clearly some meanings of *materialism* do conflict with Christianity. For example, being a materialist in the sense of caring inordinately about material wealth and possessions is contrary to Christian teaching. Moreover, some people take *materialism* to mean that there are no supernatural beings of any kind, which obviously conflicts with Christianity's claim that God exists as well as other immaterial beings such as angels and demons. Some philosophers take *materialism* to mean that all mental states, such as beliefs, desires, pains, tickles, and so forth, are nothing but brain states or other physical states. Note that the materialist view concerning human persons is not committed to any of these other forms of materialism. So a materialist view about human persons can reject the desire for inordinate material wealth, can believe that God and other supernatural beings exist, and can believe that mental states are more than just brain states. What it does claim is that human persons are material things of some sort.

Biblical scholars debate whether the Bible teaches dualism or materialism. Since the Bible is not a book on metaphysics, our view is that it does not clearly teach either one, and that it says some things that are amenable to dualists and other things that are amenable to materialists. We also need to be careful not to impose other claims on Christian

---

1. The term *four-dimensionalism* is ambiguous. It can be used to mean a view in which the past, present, and future are all equally real (and this view is sometimes called *eternalism*). It can also be used to mean that human beings persist by having temporal parts at different times in which they exist (and this view is sometimes called a *temporal-parts view*). And it can be used to mean the conjunction of eternalism and a temporal-parts view.

dualism or Christian materialism. For example, a popular version of dualism can be traced back to Plato, who presumably believed that the soul is by its very nature immortal and that the body is bad or like a prison that we need to escape (though knowing what exactly Plato believed is notoriously difficult, so this description of Plato's thought may not even be accurate). However, many Christians do not believe that the soul is naturally immortal but must be supernaturally sustained by God in order to exist forever; and Christians believe that the body and the material world are good since God created them and declared what he had made "good." Contrary to Platonic thought, the body is not bad, rather separation from the body—which is the traditional definition of death—is what is bad, for it is the consequence of sin (Rom. 6:23).

STAGES OF RESURRECTION

Depending on one's view of human nature and eschatology, common views of the resurrection often involve either three stages or two stages. The traditional Christian view has been to adopt dualism and a three-stage approach to resurrection. Right now we live in stage 1, which is our current premortem existence. At death we enter into stage 2, where we will exist in a temporary disembodied state, which many call the *intermediate state*. Finally, in stage 3 Christ will return, our bodies will be raised from the dead, and our souls will be reunited with our bodies. In the last days, when God will make everything right and make "all things new" (see Rev. 21:5), this will include our own bodies. We were meant to have bodies. Because of sin, we will die and be separated from our bodies. Though this should have been a bad thing, Christ's own death took away the sting of death (1 Cor. 15:55), and so we can be confident that while away from the body, we will be at home with the Lord (2 Cor. 5:8). However, we are not meant to stay in that immaterial state forever, and so God will reunite our souls with our resurrected bodies—and this is true for all humans (John 5:29; Acts 24:15).

While this is the traditional picture, which accords with most Protestant, Catholic, and Orthodox views, not every Christian has held to this account. Some appear to accept a two-stage approach. In short, this view eliminates stage 2. So we are in stage 1 prior to our death. When we die, there is a period of time in which we are not in existence. Then in stage 3, Christ returns and our bodies are resurrected, and we come into existence again. Under this view, there is a temporal gap in our existence—that is, a period of time in which we do not exist. This fits naturally with a materialist view of the resurrection, although, as we will see, not every Christian materialist will want to accept this two-stage approach, at least not without some qualification or modifications.

SAME BODY?

Will the resurrected body be the same one as the body we have now? We can be sure that the resurrected body will have some radically different features. For one, it will be imperishable, unlike our current bodies, which are perishable. It appears that our resurrected bodies will "shine like the sun" (Matt. 13:43), will be extremely agile since they will be "raised in power" (1 Cor. 15:43), and will be incapable of sickness and decay since they are imperishable (1 Cor. 15:42). Even Jesus's resurrected and glorified body had some unusual features. According to John 20:19–26, Jesus was able to enter into a room with no open doors (a feature of resurrected bodies that some theologians call *subtlety*). If Christ is the model or firstfruits of the resurrection, then our resurrected bodies will likely have some extraordinary characteristics too.

But will the body that goes into the grave or is cremated be the very same body that gets resurrected—that is, will the premortem body and the resurrected body be identical to each other? Not everyone agrees. Some have claimed that our resurrected bodies will be numerically distinct from our original bodies. Scripture teaches that we will receive spiritual and incorruptible bodies, and some believe that those bodies are not the exact same ones we have now. One reason for thinking that the resurrected body will not be identical to the earthly body is that it is very difficult to conceive how the earthly body could be brought back into existence, especially if it has been completely destroyed, say through cremation or in an explosion. Dualists about human persons appear to have an easier way of dealing with survival after death—for as long as the soul continues to exist, then so does the person. So if a human person acquires a brand-new resurrected body, there is no need to answer how the exact same body can be brought back into existence.

Some materialists also agree that the exact same body is not required for resurrection. The constitution view mentioned earlier is a materialist view that claims that human persons are material objects but are not identical to their bodies; rather, human persons are constituted by their bodies in a way similar to a statue that is constituted by a lump of clay.[2] What makes a human person the same person over time is having the same first-person perspective. Under this view, human persons can be constituted by different bodies, and so at the resurrection, a human person will be constituted by a glorified, imperishable body that is distinct from the earthly body. But we end up with the same human person because the glorified person has the same first-person perspective as the premortem person. So the belief that the resurrection involves a brand-new body is compatible with both dualism and materialism.

There are, however, some concerns for those who think that the resurrection involves acquiring a numerically distinct body from the original body. For one, such a view may have some difficulty in explaining what the difference would be between resurrection and reincarnation. In reincarnation people receive new bodies. What, then,

---

2. See Lynne Rudder Baker, "Death and the Afterlife," in *The Oxford Handbook of Philosophy of Religion*, ed. William J. Wainwright (Oxford: Oxford University Press, 2005). For a fuller defense of the constitution view, see Baker, *Persons and Bodies: A Constitution View* (Cambridge: Cambridge University Press, 2000).

would distinguish that from resurrection? Perhaps the difference is that resurrection is permanent in that resurrected bodies will never die, whereas reincarnated bodies will eventually die and so have to repeat the cycle of disembodiment and another reincarnation and so on. There are, of course, other salient differences; for example, resurrection occurs on earth (i.e., the new earth), whereas many reincarnation views allow for embodiment in other realms.

Even if this is an adequate way of distinguishing between resurrection and reincarnation, there are other reasons to believe that the resurrected body will be numerically identical to the original body. First, most of the early Christian fathers were dualists about human persons and yet believed that the resurrected body would be numerically identical to the original, earthly body. Second, Jesus's resurrection is often taken to be the model for the general resurrection, especially since Paul is clear that Christ's resurrection is the "firstfruits" of our resurrection (1 Cor. 15:20–23). Since the body that was laid in the tomb was identical to the one that left the tomb, many Christians affirm that at the resurrection the risen bodies will be identical to the ones we have now (though with different qualitative features).

So whether dualists or materialists, many Christians believe that the general resurrection of the dead will involve the numerically same bodies of human persons. For a dualist and a proponent of the constitution view, while human persons could survive without their original bodies, they may be theologically committed to believing in resurrected bodies that are numerically identical to the original, earthly bodies. Other versions of materialism, such as animalism or brainism, require resurrection of the same human body or same brain in order for that human person to come back into existence.

But having the same body in the resurrection raises some serious puzzles. When we die, our bodies undergo slow decay, with the atoms that make up the body being scattered. Some people are even cremated, and some Christian martyrs were burned. It is hard to see how God could bring back in the resurrection the exact same body that was once destroyed. Christians believe in bodily resurrection on the basis of revelation. But revelation does not tell us *how* resurrection will take place. So Christian philosophers have attempted to explain how God could bring back the same body. We say "could" because most of these philosophers do not think that God is limited to what we can come up with in our human minds. The resurrection is one of those Christian mysteries we will never fully understand, and the resources that God can use are far beyond what we can conceive or imagine.

By faith, we believe in the resurrection. But as we have been reiterating throughout this book, Christian thinkers have kept the motto "faith seeking understanding." So Christian philosophers have offered possible explanations for how God *could* bring back the same body, even if this is not the way God will *actually* do it. What these efforts aim to do is to show that the resurrection of the same body is logically possible, and such efforts have apologetic value in showing unbelievers that Christian belief in the resurrection (of the same body) is not irrational or incoherent. So take the following accounts of how resurrection occurs as "just-so" stories, that is, descriptions of possible ways God will resurrect our bodies.

Resurrection by Reassembly

One of the earliest proposals—which we will call *resurrection by reassembly*—was endorsed by the early church fathers, including the great philosophical theologian Augustine (354–430). We know that at death the body decays and many of its parts, such as its atoms, will be scattered. How could God bring this body back? Well, consider this scenario: You drop your watch off at a repair shop and the repairman takes the watch apart, with its parts scattered across the desk, and leaves it in that condition for a week. At the end of the week, the repairman reassembles the watch out of the parts on the desk. You might be inclined to believe that when the repairman returns the watch to you, the rightful owner, the watch you now hold is the same watch you dropped off a week ago. Had the repairman used completely different parts to assemble a watch, you would instead believe that such a watch was numerically distinct from the original watch. So it seems that what accounts for the sameness of material objects is to take the exact same parts of an object and reassemble those parts into its original form. Similarly, if God were to reassemble all the parts, such as the atoms, that made up a body right before death, then God can resurrect that same body.

Although this process seems to work for things like a watch, it becomes much more complicated when considering human bodies. Human bodies, like all other complex organisms, such as trees and puppies, are constantly changing parts. We eat, drink, breathe, and so take in new matter. We also excrete old materials, such as waste products, hair, and dead skin cells. Physicists tell us that the atoms that compose us are constantly being swapped out for other atoms, and hence the atoms that compose us now are all different from the atoms that composed us ten years ago.

This complication led to a concern that early Christian theologians noticed: What would happen if a cannibal were to eat a human victim and then immediately die? Since the atoms that made up the victim now partially make up the cannibal, how is God supposed to bring back both of them? And which body would get which atoms? If you used those atoms to make up the victim's body, would the cannibal have some weird holes in his body? The problem isn't primarily about cannibalism; the problem is that human bodies change their parts over time. And the old parts scatter and sometimes make up other bodies. Hence, it is possible that the atoms that once composed Abraham Lincoln's body right before he died will compose Eric's body right before he dies. Then how could God resurrect Lincoln's body and Eric's body?

Some might think that there is an easy and obvious solution to this problem: God does not have to use the atoms that will compose our bodies right before we die. God could use any of the atoms that composed one's body during her lifetime. That seems to make some sense, but this leads to yet another problem. Suppose at the resurrection God uses the atoms that composed your body right before you died and reassembles a body. But suppose God also uses the atoms that composed your body when you were ten years old and reassembles another body. And it seems that there is a completely different collection of atoms that made up your body at ten and that will make up your body right before you die. By the proposed solution, both of those bodies would be equally good candidates for being your body. But they both cannot be your body; there is, after all, only *one* body. And so we have to conclude that neither one is your body.[3]

The problem isn't that God would be acting mischievously. So it will not help to merely say that God would not do such a thing. What this example shows is that taking some of the old atoms and reassembling them is just not enough to resurrect the same body.

Lastly, the reason why this approach is often dismissed is because some philosophers think that you can't bring something back once it has been totally destroyed. Suppose you have a baseball signed by Hank Aaron, and it is your favorite earthly treasure. Now suppose Wesley destroys it by accidentally dropping it into a fire, and it burns away into tiny pieces of ashes. Wesley freaks out and buys some old baseballs and tries to forge the signature, but they all look like fakes. So Wesley begins to pray, asking God to bring back the baseball. Suppose that God, taking mercy on Wesley, decides to help and so takes the ashes and makes a baseball that looks exactly like the original one, signature and all. Did God bring back the original baseball? It's not obvious either way. Some philosophers think that God did bring it back; but many others think that it is not the same baseball. What God did was bring back a new baseball that is an exact replica or duplicate. But it is not the same baseball that Hank Aaron signed; it's not even Hank Aaron's signature—it's a forgery by God! This example attempts to illustrate the alleged impossibility of bringing something back once it has been totally destroyed.

---

3. This and the other objections we are discussing in this section against the resurrection-by-reassembly view were raised by Peter van Inwagen, "The Possibility of Resurrection," in Van Inwagen, *The Possibility of Resurrection and Other Essays in Christian Apologetics* (Boulder, CO: Worldview, 1998).

Some philosophers argue that these intuitions provide reasons to believe that something cannot go out of existence for a period of time and then be brought back into existence. Having a period of time where one does not exist and then comes back into existence has been called a *temporal gap*, and those who think that the ball is not the original one signed by Hank Aaron often claim that objects cannot survive a temporal gap. After all, how could something have two beginnings?

So if a human body were to be totally destroyed, it could not be brought back. And if God is going to resurrect our bodies, he can't just reassemble the old atoms. He will have to do something else. Or so the argument goes.

The Body-Snatching View

Those philosophers who think you can't bring something back once it has been destroyed often claim that a thing stays the same over time as long as there is some *continuity* (of the right sort). Eric's body when he was five years old and his body now have many different features. His body now is much taller and much heavier. Furthermore, the atoms that made up his body when he was five years old are not the same as the atoms that currently make up his body. But that five-year-old body and his body now are identical. So it seems that having the same atoms doesn't matter for bodily sameness. Rather, the way that Eric's body is now is a result of the way his body was just a moment ago and the biological or physical processes that were occurring at that time. Disrupt that bodily continuity and you annihilate the body.

If bodily sameness requires the right kind of bodily continuity, then it seems that God cannot allow the body to be totally destroyed if he intends to resurrect it. So what could God do to ensure resurrection? Remember that most philosophers don't think these proposals will be the way God *actually* resurrects bodies. Rather, these proposals are meant to show that it is *possible* for God to do so.

One radical proposal that has received much attention by philosophers is the suggestion that at the moment of death, God snatches the body and immediately replaces it with a simulacrum—that is, with an exact duplicate.[4] God takes the original body (which is either barely alive or dead but not destroyed) and preserves it somewhere. The exact duplicate left behind is what is regarded as the corpse and is the thing that gets buried or cremated. At the resurrection, God will take the original preserved body and restore it back to life, as well as endow it with whatever other features glorified bodies will have.

While some might find this proposal outrageous, this view does allow for the possibility of bodily sameness while maintaining bodily continuity between the earthly body and the resurrected body. So it does not have to deal with the problem of a temporal gap in our existence, which was raised against the resurrection-by-reassembly view.

But even so, there are some concerns with the body-snatching model of the resurrection. First, it appears that God would be involved with some trickery by letting people believe that they are seeing the same body at a funeral when in fact what they are seeing is a duplicate. Perhaps God does that because he wants us to take death seriously or because he wants us to have some remnant for symbolic or memorial reasons. But many are concerned that this kind of deception is not consistent with God's moral nature, and hence "body snatching" is not a possible way for God to preserve bodies.

Another concern is a storage problem: Where does God keep all the nearly dead bodies that are awaiting resurrection? Given the vast size of the universe, having enough space is not going to be a problem. But it is weird to think that there might be billions of bodies stacked on the other side of the Andromeda galaxy. This oddity does not show this view to be impossible, but we think that accounts of the resurrection that do not require such oddities are theoretically superior (and it could even be empirically confirmed if humans ever construct technology that allows exploration of every part of our universe).

Perhaps one way of diminishing these concerns over this body-

---

4. Van Inwagen, "The Possibility of Resurrection."

snatching theory is by supposing that God doesn't have to snatch the whole body but some part of it. One suggestion is intimated in 1 Corinthians 15:37, where God need only take the "naked kernel" or a "bare seed," which presumably would be a very small part of the human body. Perhaps preserving that small part of the body might be enough to maintain the right kind of continuity. However, we worry whether bodily continuity is even the right criterion for the persistence of human persons, and so we reject this view not for its oddities or for theological reasons but because of our metaphysical commitments.

The Falling-Elevator Account

Some may hesitate to embrace the body-snatching view while still thinking that bodily continuity is required for bodily sameness in the resurrection. Another much discussed approach has been dubbed the *falling-elevator account,* which is based on old cartoons where a character is able to survive a falling elevator by jumping out of it right before it crashes into the ground.[5]

Similarly, imagine that right before you die, God causes every single atom in your body to split in the way that amoebas do, thereby producing two successor atoms. One collection of these atoms will compose one body that will be at the place you just were right before you died, and that body will be dead. The other collection will "jump" in time and space to whenever and wherever the resurrection occurs, and that body will be revived and restored by God.[6] There are now two bodies that are candidates for being identical to the original body. But the body that is located at the place where you were right before you died is a corpse, whereas the body that "jumped" to the resurrection is alive and well. So the only candidate for being the same body is the living one, and hence God resurrected you by allowing you to "jump out" right

---

5. Dean Zimmerman, "The Compatibility of Materialism and Survival: The 'Falling Elevator' Model," *Faith and Philosophy* 16 (1999): 194–212.
6. It is crucial for this theory that the persistence conditions for human persons require immanent causal continuity, and that such causal continuity can span a temporal gap.

before you die. And this resurrected body maintains the right kind of continuity with the original body.

Like the body-snatching proposal, the falling-elevator account is merely an attempt to show that bodily resurrection is possible. There are no doubt some oddities and concerns, but its advantage is that it does not require God snatching bodies or potentially deceiving us by leaving a simulacrum. However, it does require that God endow atoms with the power to split into two successor atoms, and some might find that strange (but not impossible given God's omnipotence). It also requires that the right kind of continuity can hold even though it jumps across space and time (thereby fitting quite nicely with the two-stage model of resurrection), but one might be concerned about whether such continuity could be maintained across that span.

The main concern raised against this view, however, is that bodily sameness depends on what happens to something else besides the original body and the resurrected body. Suppose that after the split, both bodies—the one located where the original body was and the other one that jumped into the future—stayed alive. Then it looks like we have two bodies that are continuous with the original body. But we can't say that both of them are identical to the original body (since there is only one original body), and so we would have to say that neither of them is. Thus, whether you survive as the "jumped" body depends on whether there is another living body that is continuous with the original one. If there is, then you do not survive. If there isn't, then you do survive. But it is strange that whether you survive depends on what happens to some other body distant in time and space.

Some philosophers believe that whether a person at one time—for example, Eric right now—is identical to a person at another time—for example, the resurrected Eric—should depend only on features pertaining to right-now Eric and resurrected Eric. So many philosophers argue that the falling-elevator account violates what has been called the *only-x-and-y principle*, which claims that whether x is identical to y cannot depend on anything other than the intrinsic features of x and y. But the falling-elevator model makes Eric's survival depend on something external to right-now Eric and resurrected Eric, namely, the corpse that is causally continuous with right-now Eric. If that corpse were to survive, then resurrected Eric would not be identical to right-now Eric, which violates the only-*x*-and-*y* principle. So those who are committed on the basis of metaphysical considerations into accepting the only-*x*-and-*y* principle will naturally reject the falling-elevator view. However, others think that perhaps a person's survival depends on something external—in fact, we have suggested that the will of God may be that extra external factor that human survival depends on, which we will say more about later.

Uninformative Answer

So far the last two views agree that there can be no disruption or temporal gaps between the earthly body and the resurrected body. Whatever way God brings a body back, he will have to maintain continuity of some kind. However, some philosophers have questioned whether this is right. Instead, they think that continuity is not required; there can be temporal gaps or disruptions in our existence. This much they agree with the resurrection-by-reassembly view. Yet many of these philosophers reject resurrection by reassembly. So how can God bring back the same body in the resurrection? Well, one proposal is to say that there is no real answer to that question. You cannot say God will do it by gathering all of your old atoms and reassembling them. Nor can you say that God will do it by ensuring the right kind of continuity, either by body snatching or by having all of your atoms split into two. According to this view, when we say someone at one time is the same person as someone else at another time, there is no informative answer to give as to why or how that is the case. This view in philosophy is sometimes called *anti-criterialism*, because it says that there are no criteria for our identity over time.[7] Perhaps one could give necessary

---

7. Trenton Merricks, "How to Live Forever without Saving Your Soul: Physicalism and Immortality," in *Soul, Body, and Survival*, ed. Kevin Corcoran (Ithaca, NY: Cornell University Press, 2001).

conditions for human persistence, or perhaps even sufficient conditions. But what they can't do is give informative necessary and sufficient conditions. So, if someone were to give necessary and sufficient conditions, they would be uninformative, much like saying, "What makes a person in 1985 identical to another person in 2015 is that they are identical"—but that wouldn't be helpful or informative at all.

So, if in fact Eric-now is identical to resurrected Eric, then they are the same and that's that! No complicated story needs to be given, and hence no worry about where God is keeping nearly dead bodies or requiring that we "jump" into the future to survive. To be clear, this isn't to say that philosophy is to be given up. In fact, this is a philosophical view. It says there are no informative answers to the question of bodily sameness (or perhaps to any question about identity over time). It is one of those basic facts that you cannot further analyze. Your resurrected body will be the same as your body now, and no further analysis can be provided.

Although this might seem appealing at first, this approach still raises some concerns. It is strange that no account or criterion can be given for the persistence of human persons. We might then get it wrong whether someone persisted over time. Of course, a quick retort is that many of the things we use now to determine whether we are dealing with the same person (e.g., psychological continuity, biological continuity) can still be used as evidence to figure out who someone is. But now suppose that God resurrects a body and claims that it is the same body as the earthly body. Of course, since God is omniscient, he will not be wrong. But he would not be able to explain it to us. He might just say, "It's the same one; trust me." And of course we would trust him and believe it is the same one. But it is weird to think that there is *nothing* that God could say or do to explain *how* it is the same one. He could not explain it even to angels, because there is nothing to explain.

And imagine if there were two indistinguishable bodies (that is, you could not tell them apart no matter how closely you examined them, even with microscopes or with fancy technology). Both of them could not be the same as the original body, but if one of them were the same, God would know and he could tell us. Yet many think it is counterintuitive that there is no reason in principle to be given to explain which one is the original one—at least no reason to give other than just saying, "That's the same as the original body." Many philosophers find it preferable that we should be able in principle to analyze what makes one body at one time be the same as another body at a different time. Even if having the same parts or having the right kind of continuity are wrong, many think we should not yet concede but should keep trying to provide an informative answer. And it doesn't have to be completely informative, but at least more so than the proposal suggested here.

METAPHYSICS AND RESURRECTION

In this section we will present some underexplored approaches to the resurrection, ones that we take to be promising or interesting lines of inquiry. But because they enter into some technical areas of philosophy, such as metaphysics, this section will merely provide a brief summary.

One such approach has historical pedigree and until recently had been ignored by many philosophers; but it has recently seen a revival by contemporary philosophers and theologians. This is the view of Thomas Aquinas, who endorsed a theory of human persons that is often known as *hylomorphism*, which we considered in chapter 3 in our discussion of the Trinity.[8] Hylomorphism can be traced even further back to Aristotle. The term comes from two Greek words, *hylē*, which means "matter," and *morphē*, which means "form." According to hylomorphism, human persons are comprised of form and matter. It is

---

8. For an in-depth and helpful discussion of Aquinas's hylomorphism, see Eleonore Stump's chapter "Forms and Bodies: The Soul," in her book *Aquinas* (New York: Routledge, 2003). For Aquinas's hylomorphic approach to the resurrection, see Stump, "Resurrection and the Separated Soul," in *The Oxford Handbook of Aquinas*, ed. Brian Davies and Eleonore Stump (Oxford: Oxford University Press, 2014).

quite difficult to say what exactly form and matter are supposed to be (and many philosophers do not agree); however, Aquinas (following Aristotle) called the forms of human beings their "soul."

Aquinas's view of the soul is fairly complicated—the way you think about the soul is probably not how he thought about it. Although Aquinas thought the soul was immaterial, it appeared to him to be closer to the organization or configuration of an object. Does that mean Aquinas counts as a dualist? It is difficult to say. If he was a dualist, he did not fit the typical bill, especially since he did not think of the soul as a separate, complete substance in the way that typical dualists often hold. Moreover, he said things that made him sound as though he were a materialist, especially since he identified the human person with the living organism (and hence appeared to hold to an animalist version of materialism). However, Aquinas also does not fit neatly into the materialist camp, because he accepted that souls can exist disembodied.

While it is difficult to interpret Aquinas with regard to his hylomorphism, it is at least usually agreed upon that Aquinas accepted the claim that the human person is not identical to the soul. In fact, many think of the soul as a (proper) part of the person. Moreover, what makes a living body the same thing over time is that it possesses the same soul over time, for the soul that organizes your body now can organize some matter later, thereby making that matter be your body. Finally, Aquinas held that the soul can survive when separated from matter. So, to take a hylomorphic approach to resurrection would be to follow the three-stage approach and claim that the substantial form survives in stage 2, and in stage 3 the soul reinforms matter, thereby bringing back the original living body (but with its new, glorified characteristics).

Perhaps the main debate among those who endorse a hylomorphic approach to resurrection is to ask about stage 2, in particular whether the original person can survive with only their soul in the intermediate state. Some claim that human persons can survive with their soul as their only part (even if they are not identical to their soul), and these philosophers are often called *survivalists*. However, others think that the person does not survive in stage 2 but that only the soul does, and since human persons are not identical to the soul, merely having a soul does not guarantee the existence of the person. Philosophers who hold this view are often called *corruptionists*. For the corruptionist, the human person goes out of existence during stage 2 but then comes back into existence when the soul reanimates matter in stage 3. Scholars debate whether Aquinas was a survivalist or a corruptionist, and they also debate which one should be regarded as true, independent of what Aquinas himself believed.

While hylomorphism has increased in popularity and attention recently, it is still not a widely held view. So someone might argue that the acceptance of hylomorphism is unnecessary, preferring to stay instead with a typical form of dualism or materialism. However, contemporary philosophers have offered a lot of reasons to take hylomorphism seriously, especially for considerations independent of theological concerns. For example, some philosophers argue that hylomorphism is the best way to understand the nature of parts and wholes, and others argue that it is the best way to analyze material objects generally. Moreover, philosophical theologians have also utilized a hylomorphic approach to help understand other Christian doctrines too, such as the incarnation[9] and, as we have seen, the Trinity.

Another interesting development is that a few philosophical theologians today have tried to revive resurrection by reassembly, and while we do not endorse that approach, we do think it is not as implausible as some have suggested. We think that resurrection by reassembly can be made even more plausible if it is combined with the claim that God's will is a necessary condition for the persistence of objects as well as when objects come to be made up of other objects.[10] To state it metaphorically, the will of God is the glue of the world—it holds

---

9. Michael Rea, "Hylomorphism and the Incarnation," in *The Metaphysics of the Incarnation*, ed. Anna Marmodoro and Jonathan Hill (Oxford: Oxford University Press, 2011).

10. Eric T. Yang and Stephen T. Davis, "Composition and the Will of God: Reconsidering Resurrection by Reassembly," in *Paradise Understood: New Philosophical Essays about Heaven*, ed. T. Ryan Byerly and Eric J. Silverman (Oxford: Oxford University Press, 2017).

objects together over time and holds objects together at some time to make up a further object. This view fits nicely with those who want to hold to a strong view of divine conservation, which is the theological claim that God sustains in existence the world and all of its contents. Objects lack "existential inertia"—they would cease to exist were it not for God sustaining them in existence. So not only is God the creator of the world, but God is the sustainer of the world.

Now suppose that for there to be a body, there cannot simply be some atoms arranged in a bodily shape—God also has to will that there be a body (if not, then all we would have are atoms arranged in a bodily shape but not an actual body). Furthermore, suppose that for you right now to be the same as you yesterday, God has to will that you be the same. Perhaps there also has to be the right continuity relations (or perhaps not), but those relations will not be enough—God must also will that you be the same; otherwise you end up with a mere duplicate.

Although we do not accept resurrection by reassembly, we think that such a proponent should claim that God resurrects the same body as the premortem body if a sufficient number of particles that once made up the premortem body are suitably arranged, and if God wills that there be a human body made up of those particles and also wills that the resultant human body made up of those particles be identical to the premortem body. Once these two divine volitions are brought into the picture, the proponent of resurrection by reassembly can avoid several of the objections raised earlier against it. For example, consider the objection of ending up with two bodies, one made up of the same atoms right before you die and the other made up of the atoms when you were ten. Now God can only will that either one of the collection of atoms compose a body or one of the bodies be the same as the original one. That is, at most, God could will only one of those things if he intends to resurrect you. And since most philosophical theologians claim that omnipotence requires only being able to do what is logically possible, we take it that this would not undermine God's omnipotence.

There is, no doubt, a significant cost to this approach. Similar to the falling-elevator view, it necessitates that sameness of person over time, as well as composition, requires something external. In this case, the external factor is not a potential candidate for being the original person; rather, the external factor is God's will. So, like the falling-elevator view, a view that requires divine volitions for a human person to persist over time will violate the only-x-and-y principle. We think, though, that for those who take divine conservation seriously, rejecting the only-x-and-y principle may not be very disconcerting.

Finally, some have engaged in technical metaphysical issues to rework the conception of resurrection. For example, some think that we should think of survival not in terms of being identical over time but in terms of having temporal parts over time—and so we should think of ourselves as four-dimensional space-time "worms." That is, we are spread across time, just like we are spread across space. So, my earthly body and my resurrected body are not the same. Rather, they are both temporal parts of me, where I am the thing that is spread across time. And so I never exist wholly at one time, only partly at each time—just as I never exist wholly at one tiny spatial point but am spread across space. Resurrection occurs when there is a later temporal part that occurs in stage 3 that is a part of a person who has temporal parts in stage 1. Of course, philosophers strongly debate whether human persons persist over time by being wholly present at each time they exist (so that one person at a time is numerically identical to a person at another time), or whether human persons persist by having temporal parts at different times in which they exist.

Others focus on the notion of location in space-time regions or on the concept of hypertime to make sense of the resurrection.[11] According to the latter approach, resurrection does not occur in the future—within our universe, which can be conceived as a four-dimensional space-time block. Instead, the concept of hypertime, a temporal plane

11. Hud Hudson, "The Resurrection and Hypertime," in *Paradise Understood: New Philosophical Essays about Heaven*, ed. T. Ryan Byerly and Eric J. Silverman (Oxford: Oxford University Press, 2017).

above our own time, is employed. Some argue that we need such a notion to make sense of the "flow" of time. One proposal of the resurrection takes different hypertimes to have different content, some having four-dimensional space-time blocks (i.e., universes) and perhaps some having no content at all. So all of the times that we experience may occur in a single hypertime. However, resurrection may be construed as not occurring in the future but in the hyperfuture—a hypermoment distinct from the hypermoment that our universe currently occupies. Clearly, metaphysical inquiry can open up a whole host of different ways of conceptualizing the resurrection, and we think that these discussions show the potential for much fruitful investigation into understanding how the general resurrection could work.

CONCLUDING THOUGHTS

Again, Christians can affirm by faith that God will resurrect our bodies in the last days. But Christians with faith who are seeking understanding will want to understand *how* resurrection is possible. We have explored some proposals and also raised some concerns for each view. This means the discussion doesn't end here. Perhaps readers will think one of these views is worth defending and so will have to consider how to respond to some of the concerns raised against that view. Perhaps others will come up with another explanation or account. What theory is produced will likely depend on how one answers several metaphysical questions or on which substantive metaphysical assumptions one adopts—and therefore theorizing about the resurrection requires having a good handle on the philosophical concepts.

Plenty more thinking, praying, reflecting, and discussing needs to be done about the resurrection. Philosophers would be wise to listen to the voice of Christians who are experts in other areas (especially biblical exegetes, systematic theologians, historical theologians, and the like), working together in community to understand the faith that has been revealed to us. In this chapter we have shared some of the philosophical insights, and we hope that readers will reflect deeply and share their insights, and that as a church body we will all grow together.

FURTHER READINGS

For a good overview of many of the themes discussed in this chapter as well as some of the biblical, historical, and theological issues pertaining to the resurrection, see Stephen T. Davis, *Risen Indeed: Making Sense of the Resurrection* (Grand Rapids: Eerdmans, 1993); and Stephen T. Davis, Daniel Kendall, SJ, and Gerald O'Collins, SJ, eds., *The Resurrection* (Oxford: Oxford University Press, 1997).

For the case for numerically distinct resurrected bodies, see Stephen T. Davis, "Traditional Christian Belief in the Resurrection of the Body," *New Scholasticism* 62 (1988): 72–97, on the dualist position; and see Lynne Rudder Baker, "Death and the Afterlife," in *The Oxford Handbook of Philosophy of Religion*, ed. William J. Wainwright (Oxford: Oxford University Press, 2005), on the constitution view.

For a critique of the resurrection-by-reassembly view and a presentation of the body-snatching view, see Peter van Inwagen's influential chapter "The Possibility of Resurrection" in his book *The Possibility of Resurrection and Other Essays in Christian Apologetics* (Boulder, CO: Worldview, 1998). The falling-elevator account comes from Dean Zimmerman, "The Compatibility of Materialism and Survival: The 'Falling Elevator' Model," *Faith and Philosophy* 16 (1999): 194–212. The rejection of an informative answer is defended in Trenton Merricks's "How to Live Forever without Saving Your Soul: Physicalism and Immortality," in *Soul, Body, and Survival*, ed. Kevin Corcoran (Ithaca, NY: Cornell University Press, 2001). See also Merricks's chapter "The Resurrection of the Body and the Life Everlasting," in *Reason for the Hope Within*, ed. M. Murray (Grand Rapids: Eerdmans, 1999).

For a study of Aquinas's view of resurrection, a good place to start is Eleonore Stump, "Resurrection, Reassembly, and Reconstitution: Aquinas on the Soul," in *Die menschliche Seele: Brauchen wir den Dualismus?* ed. B. Niederbacher and E. Runggaldier (Frankfurt: Ontos Verlag, 2006). We also recommend Patrick Toner, "On Hylomorphism and Personal Identity," *European Journal of Philosophy* 19 (2011): 454–73, for some discussion on the survivalist-corruptionist debate (Stump endorses survivalism, whereas Toner endorses corruptionism).

Also check out Ryan Byerly and Eric Silverman's *Paradise Understood: New Philosophical Essays about Heaven* (Oxford: Oxford University Press, 2017). This book includes chapters on Aquinas's view of resurrection, discussion of time and resurrection, and our chapter that defends resurrection by reassembly by incorporating God's will in a theory of composition and persistence. Another helpful volume of papers on the metaphysics of the resurrection is Georg Gasser, ed., *Personal Identity and Resurrection: How Do We Survive Our Death?* (Burlington, VT: Ashgate, 2010).

HEAVEN AND HELL

Christians have traditionally believed that the final end for all human beings will be one of two places: heaven or hell. Popular images are associated with heaven and hell, some of which come from the Bible—such as streets of gold (Rev. 21:21) and an everlasting fire (Rev. 20:10)—and some from popular imagination, such as people with harps on clouds and demons with pitchforks. Many theologians do not take all of the biblical descriptions literally but rather take them to be expressions of how wonderful heaven will be and how horrible hell will be. In a more technical sense, heaven is eternal union with God, and hell is eternal separation from God.

If we take a traditional approach to life after death, human beings are temporarily disembodied after death, existing during a period often called the *intermediate state*. When Christ returns, our bodies will be resurrected and the blessed will live with God, whereas the damned will be separated from God. For most Protestant Christians, the souls of the blessed enjoy union with God during the intermediate state, especially since Scripture claims that at death we will be "away from the body and at home with the Lord" (2 Cor. 5:8). If heaven is union with God, then the blessed are "in heaven" during the intermediate state and the resurrected state (or stages 2 and 3 from the previous chapter). Some theologians have used "heaven" to refer merely to the intermediate state, but heaven is usually regarded as the final destination for God's people, and so it is much more fitting to take "heaven" as referring to the periods after death in which we will be united with God. For most Protestants, then, Christians will be in heaven immediately after death. Catholics and even some Protestants also believe in purgatory, a period of cleansing usually situated during the intermediate state. So for believers in purgatory, the redeemed do not enter into heaven until the resurrection or until they are completely purified in the intermediate state. In this chapter we will focus on several philosophical concerns that arise when considering hell, heaven, and purgatory.

HELL

The traditional doctrine of hell typically involves the claim that some people will never repent and will reject God's free offer of his grace, and so they will experience everlasting misery and punishment in hell from which they can never escape. Belief in hell has been a standard part of the Christian worldview, especially given several references to hell in the Bible. Most descriptions of hell in Scripture highlight the place as one of torment, misery, and suffering. For example, the Bible describes hell as a place of eternal fire (Matt. 25:41), a place of darkness where there is weeping and gnashing of teeth (Matt. 8:12), and a place without rest (Rev. 14:11).

Many theologians throughout history have distinguished between two kinds of suffering associated with hell: the *pain of sense* and the *pain of loss*. The pain of sense is often depicted as physical or experiential suffering, such as the lick of fire scorching the bodies of the damned. The pain of loss involves the recognition that eternal happiness and the heart's deepest desire, which is union with God, is forever gone and out of reach for the denizens of hell. Most theologians throughout history appear to have accepted the claim that the pains of hell are of both types, or at least they often speak as though both types are involved. Many other theologians, however, believe that the descriptions of the pain of sense are merely metaphorical, and that the truly devastating suffering experienced in hell is the pain of loss.

Recently the doctrine of hell has fallen on hard times. A growing number of Christians have rejected it. And even for those who do accept some version of hell, it is noticeably absent in sermons and mainstream Christian dialogue. Part of the reason is the difficulty in understanding how the doctrine of hell can be compatible with a perfectly loving God. If God is perfectly loving, he will want what is best for his creation, especially his children—those who are made in his image. What is best for human beings is eternal union with God. And if God is sovereign such that all aspects of creation are under his direct control, then God should be able to make everyone eventually submit to him, and hence he should be able to save everyone. If he does not save everyone, then it appears that he does not love everyone, yet it is part of Christian doctrine to claim that God loves every single person.

In light of this concern, several Christian thinkers have abandoned the traditional doctrine of hell. Some deny it by rejecting any conception of hell or everlasting suffering. Others maintain the heart of the doctrine but revise or modify the traditional conception in significant ways. What is interesting is that many of these alterations to the traditional doctrine appeal to the Bible in support of their position. In what follows, we provide a survey of some of the main options that are currently being discussed.

Some philosophical theologians have defended the traditional doctrine, while stressing that much of the popular imagery is a caricature of the traditional view. Many traditional proponents defend the theme that hell is a place of punishment. Of the different theories of punishment, perhaps the most salient one is *retributive punishment*—that the guilty deserve to be punished. Those who have sinned against God stand guilty and therefore deserve to be punished. But why does the punishment have to be everlasting? After all, their crimes appear to be finite, and yet they must endure an infinite duration of punishment, and this appears difficult to square with the view that God is completely just and fair. Some have responded by suggesting that the rejection of God is no mere finite crime or wrongdoing but egregious enough to merit everlasting punishment. Many others believe that the denizens of hell deserve only finite punishment, but their continued rejection of God deserves punishment, and since they continue to reject God forever, they deserve their punishment forever.

Many Christians, however, have tried to maintain the heart of the traditional view while rejecting the focus on punishment. Rather, the focus is placed on the fact that the denizens of hell choose to be separated from God. That is, they are freely choosing to be separated, and God is granting what they want. This idea was popularized by C. S. Lewis, who made the fairly well-known comment that "the damned are, in one sense, successful, rebels to the end; that the gates of hell are locked on the inside."[1] According to this approach to hell, it remains logically possible for the residents of hell to repent and to choose God. However, many who hold this view believe that there will be some who do freely choose to remain eternally separated from God, like a spoiled child who would rather pout and wreck the party than apologize and be reconciled with others. Psychologically, it seems that even when someone knows the right thing to do, they still choose to do what is wrong, even when it hurts them—perhaps out of pride or a sense of being in the right. Similarly, those in hell will never repent or apologize because they believe that they are in the right and that God is in the wrong. And so they freely choose to remain separated, and will sadly do so forever. We take this to be the most plausible version that retains much of the traditional view, but with a greater emphasis on the part of humans who repeatedly reject God.

A growing number of Christian thinkers and theologians have abandoned even the core of the traditional view, suggesting that hell either does not exist or is merely temporary. One such view is *universalism*, which in brief is the belief that all human beings will eventually be saved. Accordingly, there is either no hell, or if there is a hell, it is merely a temporary abode—but it will eventually be emptied out.

---

1. C. S. Lewis, *The Problem of Pain* (New York: Harper One, 1940), 131.

Some universalists believe that the rejection of an everlasting hell fits best with biblical teaching. For example, Paul claimed that "God was pleased to have all his fullness dwell in him, and through him to reconcile to himself all things, whether things on earth or things in heaven, by making peace through his blood, shed on the cross" (Col. 1:19–20), that "in Adam all die, so in Christ all will be made alive" (1 Cor. 15:22), and that "one righteous act resulted in justification and life for all people" (Rom. 5:18). Universalists stress the word "all" in these passages, suggesting that it refers to every human being without qualification or exception.

Proponents of the traditional view typically respond by saying that guilty offenders must be punished or are freely choosing to remain separated from God. However, several universalists have rejected the retributive theory of punishment that underlies the former approach. And other universalists claim that God would act in such a way as to override our freedom. We may be regarding our relationship with God without taking into account the size of the gap that stands between God and us.[2] Rather than thinking of the relationship between God and humans as a parent and child, the relationship is perhaps better captured by the relationship between a parent and a toddler. Toddlers have no understanding of their environment and the dangers that lurk all around them. No good parent would allow her baby to toddle around without supervision and protection, and a good parent would have no problem intervening if the child were about to undertake something that could seriously harm him. Similarly, some universalists aver that God would intervene to protect humans from great harm, the worst of harms being separation from God, even if that requires overriding their freedom.[3]

Other universalists think that God can save all people even without

2. Marilyn McCord Adams, "The Problem of Hell: A Problem of Evil for Christians," in *Reasoned Faith: Essays in Philosophical Theology in Honor of Norman Kretzmann*, ed. Eleonore Stump and Norman Kretzmann (Ithaca, NY: Cornell University Press, 1993).

3. For more on this plus related themes, see Marilyn McCord Adams, *Horrendous Evils and the Goodness of God* (Ithaca, NY: Cornell University Press, 1999).

overriding their freedom. If someone acts freely and yet is choosing to be in hell and separated from God, it seems that they are ignorant of crucial facts or are deceived about what good things are available to them. So even if someone is in hell, they will realize they are miserable, and it seems unlikely that they would continue to remain in that state, especially if there is a way out of hell for them. Moreover, if all that is missing is knowledge of such a way out, it would seem cruel for God to withhold such knowledge. Hence, God can ensure that all people, including the denizens of hell, are fully informed and free from ignorance. With full information, we might then suppose that all people would choose to be rescued from eternal misery and thereby choose God and heaven.[4] This seems especially true if one takes it that human beings have free will and are freely choosing to be in hell. If the residents of hell are choosing to be in hell, and therefore have the option of leaving, then it seems that if they are genuinely free, they will eventually choose to leave, provided that they have adequate understanding and access to all the information.

We think there are several problems for these universalist proposals. While it is true there is a huge gap between God and human beings, God has revealed himself in such a way that we are not totally ignorant of his will and his desire for our lives. And while the parent-child analogy is in Scripture, so is the marriage-spouse analogy—we are Christ's bride, one who is charged to remain faithful to her covenant promise. So it seems that human beings are not off the hook—we can be held morally responsible for our deeds.

Additionally, even if God provides full information and reasons to be rescued from hell, it seems that some people have become psychologically disposed to reject God, and so there is no feasible way for them to choose God and heaven. We see this in Scripture, especially with the Egyptian Pharaoh's confrontation with Moses and Aaron.

---

4. For such a defense of universalism, see Thomas Talbott, "A Case for Christian Universalism," in *Universal Salvation? The Current Debate*, ed. Robin A. Parry and Christopher H. Partridge (Grand Rapids: Eerdmans, 2003).

Despite the various plagues that declared who the Lord was and what the Lord was capable of doing, Pharaoh hardened his heart. Even when Pharaoh's magicians declared that the finger of God was at work (Ex. 8:19), no amount of evidence made him repent or retract. Indeed, he let them go, not because he had opened himself to God but out of defeat—his heart was still hardened, which is evident in that he later sent out an army to overtake the Israelites at the Red Sea.

A hardened heart is a will that has been formed in such a way that no amount of reasons or evidence will change the person's mind. Characters are formed by the choices we make, and we can make our characters in such a way that even if later we have no option but to act a certain way, we are still responsible for the choice we make since we are responsible for forming our characters in that way.[5] The traditional view of hell, then, can maintain that even if God gives every reason for a person to choose him and escape hell, a person's heart may be so hardened that that person defiantly rejects God's offer. We have likely all seen children and even adults choose misery over peace and joy out of pride and stubbornness ("I will never say I'm sorry!"). If someone's character has been so formed, then it does not matter if they have an infinite number of choices, for they will always choose to reject God if they stew in their pride and hatred.[6]

Universalism is not the only nontraditional approach. Another growing response is *annihilationism*, which is the view that the damned do not live forever in torment but are extinguished from existence—so only the blessed in heaven live forever. Some of the Bible passages used by proponents of annihilationism are Matthew 7:13 ("the gate . . . that leads to destruction"); Romans 9:22 ("the objects of his wrath—prepared for destruction"); and 2 Thessalonians 1:9 ("They will be punished with everlasting destruction"), where the language of

---

5. For a sophisticated defense of such a view, see Robert Kane, *The Significance of Free Will* (Oxford: Oxford University Press, 1998).

6. For further elaboration of this response, see Stephen T. Davis, "Universalism, Hell, and the Fate of the Ignorant," *Modern Theology* 6 (1990): 173–86; and Eric T. Yang and Stephen T. Davis, "Choosing Eternal Separation: Reply to Gwiazda," *Sophia* 54 (2015): 217–19.

destruction is taken literally. Similar to universalists, annihilationists assert that there is no hell or that it is only temporary. However, some annihilationists agree with the traditional view that some human beings will reject God because of their hardened hearts, and so it is not feasible to think they will ever choose God and heaven. But everlasting punishment appears cruel and unfair, especially for those who think that a finite crime does not deserve an infinite punishment—so those who choose not to be in misery may be mercifully annihilated from existence.

However, one objection that can be raised is whether someone would choose annihilation over existence. After all, some people would experience an existential dread when dwelling on the possibility of not existing. For example, the Spanish philosopher Miguel de Unamuno (1864–1936) wrote that "as a youth, and even as a child, I remained unmoved when shown the most moving pictures of hell, for even then nothing appeared to me quite so horrible as the nothingness itself." He added, "I do not want to die. . . . I want this 'I' to live—this poor 'I' that I am and that I feel myself to be here and now and therefore the problem of the duration of my soul . . . tortures me."[7] If this is right, it is hard to imagine someone choosing annihilation.

Before we conclude the discussion on hell, we want to address a typical question that arises concerning the fate of those who never heard the gospel or never had a chance to respond to God's offer of salvation. Much has been written on this, so we will not delve too deeply. However, some philosophers think that we can't know God's reasons, but that we can insist that God is fair and just. Others appeal to Molinism (which we discussed in chapter 2), where God has middle knowledge, which is the knowledge of what human beings would freely do if placed in a certain circumstance. So, it may be that God has so arranged the world that those who never hear the gospel would not

---

7. Miguel de Unamuno, *Tragic Sense of Life*, trans. J. E. Crawford Flitch (New York: Barnes & Noble, 2006), 8, 60.

have responded positively to it had they been given the opportunity to hear it.[8]

While we admit that we do not know exactly how this will be resolved by God, we think that the possibility of postmortem evangelism is a viable option that is consistent with the teachings of Scripture. That is, those who did not hear the gospel or who have not hardened their hearts may have an opportunity to receive the message and thereby choose on that basis even after death (and some appeal to the tradition of the "harrowing of hell" to back up this view).[9] Similar to the problem of evil, perhaps the most appropriate response is to provide a way of showing how it is possible for God to be good and just while dealing fairly with those who never heard, at the same time admitting that God's resources no doubt go far beyond what human beings can conceive.

PURGATORY

As we discussed in the previous chapter, the traditional view of life after death includes an intermediate state of temporary disembodiment. While there is no clear indication of what will be happening during that time, some believe that the intermediate state involves purgation for most Christians who died—that they will be situated in a period or place often referred to as "purgatory." Contrary to popular depictions, purgatory is not a middle place between heaven and hell, like a kind of limbo (which has also been inaccurately depicted in popular culture) for those who are neither good nor wicked. Rather, purgatory is a place for those who are ultimately bound for heaven but are not yet ready (and limbo is traditionally conceived as a location

8. For this view, see William Lane Craig, "'No Other Name': A Middle Knowledge Perspective on the Exclusivity of Salvation through Christ," *Faith and Philosophy* 6 (1989): 172–88.

9. For further elaboration of this response, see Stephen T. Davis, "Universalism, Hell, and the Fate of the Ignorant," *Modern Theology* 6 (1990): 173–86.

in hell, perhaps for virtuous pagans and others who were not morally vicious but did not receive God's offer of salvation). Purgatory, then, is not a final destination in the way that heaven and hell are—it is a temporary stopping place.

We now turn to the nature of purgatory, and there are two dominant conceptions: the *satisfaction view* and the *sanctification view*. The satisfaction view seems to be the more common way in which purgatory is conceived. Christians believe that the guilt of sin was forgiven by Christ's atoning work in his death on the cross and his resurrection. Although the guilt of sin is no more, the stain of sin remains and must be cleansed. If human beings were still guilty of sin, they would deserve eternal punishment. But because Christ has made satisfaction for what was owed to God, human beings can enjoy eternal union with God. However, the stains of sin leave room for temporal punishment or satisfaction that must still be made, and that is what happens to Christians in purgatory.

The sanctification view, on the other hand, focuses not on temporal punishment or penance but on spiritual growth. When we die, most of us will likely not be perfectly holy. The Holy Spirit has been sanctifying us, but the work may not have been completed on earth. If that happens, then purgatory will be the period in which the sanctifying work will be finished, and it will be at that time that human beings will be made perfect and ready to enter into heaven.

Consider the following example. Suppose a king finds a peasant who owns nothing and is living in a wretched state because he chose to do so. The peasant has violated the king's laws and so owes the king much and deserves to be thrown in jail. However, suppose the king leaves the palace and comes to the peasant and releases him from his debt, thereby removing the consequence of being imprisoned. Moreover, the king in his graciousness decides that the peasant can even live with him in the palace, and that he is designating a spare room in the palace just for the peasant. The peasant looks at his rags and his filthy face. It is easy to imagine that the peasant would desire to wash up and put on nicer clothes, especially if that's an option for him. This is one reason why C. S. Lewis, a Protestant Christian, believed in purgatory. He wrote,

> Our souls *demand* Purgatory, don't they? Would it not break the heart if God said to us, "It is true, my son, that your breath smells and your rags drip with mud and slime, but we are charitable here and no one will upbraid you with these things, nor draw away from you. Enter into the joy"? Should we not reply, "With submission, sir, and if there is no objection, I'd *rather* be cleaned first." "It may hurt, you know"—"Even so, sir."[10]

Similar to Lewis's view, some claim the placement and duration of being in purgatory is freely chosen, just as we freely choose now to participate with the Holy Spirit in his sanctifying work in our lives.

Just how different are the satisfaction view and the sanctification view of purgatory? According to some, they are not different at all.[11] While the concept of satisfaction typically focuses on penance or temporary punishment, it may be merely a difference in stress or emphasis, and at the heart of the view, there may not be any significant difference between the satisfaction view and the sanctification view.

Belief in purgatory has been predominately held by Roman Catholics, though some Protestants do accept it. Some base it on a few suggestive texts in Scripture that describe purification. For example, Malachi 3:3 says, "He will sit as a refiner and purifier of silver; he will purify the Levites and refine them like gold and silver," and 1 Corinthians 3:15 states, "If [what has been built] is burned up, the builder will suffer loss but yet will be saved—even though only as one escaping through the flames." These texts are clearly inconclusive. Some also appeal to 2 Maccabees 12:44, which mentions prayers and making atonement for

---

10. C. S. Lewis, *Letters to Malcolm: Chiefly on Prayer* (Orlando: Harcourt, 1964), chap. 20.
11. Neal Judisch, "Sanctification, Satisfaction, and the Purpose of Purgatory," *Faith and Philosophy* 26 (2009): 167–85.

the dead, which seems to imply purgatory, though most Protestants do not regard this text as authoritative since it is not part of the biblical canon. However, purgatory became an official part of Roman Catholic dogma at the Council of Lyons in 1274, and so it is an item of faith that must be believed by Roman Catholics.

Are there additional reasons for accepting purgatory, especially for Protestants? A few philosophers have offered some arguments in favor of belief in purgatory.[12] One argument focuses on the imperfect state that most Christians are in when they die. Heaven is a place where there is no sin, and so it seems that the redeemed must be perfectly holy to be with God—after all, how could people see God face-to-face if they were still in sin? The problem, however, is that most redeemed humans die as imperfect persons with moral defects and vices. Some Christians die while still struggling with temptations, and their desires are not rightly ordered. Since at the resurrection all human beings will be glorified, there is a period between death and the final resurrection where human beings are sanctified and freed from their moral defects.

A natural response to this argument would be to claim that God can make someone instantaneously holy, so that immediately after death, the redeemed are fully sanctified and made perfect, and hence they are capable of dwelling immediately with God in heaven. If instantaneous holiness can be had by the redeemed, then purgatory is unnecessary. Defenders of this argument for purgatory have responded in two ways. The first is that if sanctification can be "zapped" in such a way that someone is instantaneously sanctified, then why can't God zap us in our earthly life so that we would be instantaneously sanctified? This appears to be a modified version of the so-called problem of evil, and some of the responses to that problem may be applicable here. The source of the concern, then, appears to be whether sanctification demands a temporal process or whether it can be instantaneous, and

---

12. For the most substantive defense of purgatory, and one made by a Protestant philosopher, see Jerry Walls, *Purgatory: The Logic of Total Transformation* (Oxford: Oxford University Press, 2011).

whether a "zappy" sanctification would undermine the value of the sanctifying process.

However, there is another concern for "zappy" sanctification raised by some defenders of purgatory. Suppose that someone is zapped so as to be made instantaneously perfect; thus, they are completely perfect and without moral defect. But would that still be the same person? Imagine yourself or someone who has many temptations and sinful desires, and who often gives in to those temptations and commits sinful actions. Now imagine that in one second all of those temptations and desires are immediately gone, and instead there is in their place a whole host of holy desires and virtues that were not there before. Some are concerned that such a character transformation would be so radical that it would result in a different person, and hence it would not be "you" that was sanctified, but rather you were replaced by someone else—a better and holier version. If all of your moral defects and vices were gone and new virtues were acquired, we might suppose that it would be hard to recognize yourself as yourself.

This may not be too worrisome, however. Much depends on what it takes to be the same person over time, which philosophers have argued a lot about. Perhaps you stay the same over time as long as you have the same soul, or as long as you have memories of your past experience. If either of these two views are correct, then perhaps you could survive being zapped into perfection since you could have the same soul or remember your past experiences. However, perhaps a sanctification zap is not a threat to personal identity but a threat to the value of sanctification. Much more work needs to be done, especially on the theology of sanctification.

HEAVEN: STATIC OR DYNAMIC

Heaven is the ultimate destination for the redeemed in Christ; it is eternal union with God, the true object of our faith, hope, and love.

Because of imagery based on Revelation 21:21, heaven is often depicted in popular culture as having pearly gates and streets paved with gold. However, most Christians believe this is metaphorical for the spiritual riches contained in heaven—which is also depicted in the rest of the imagery where there is neither temple nor sun since God is the temple and the sun! In sum, heaven is the best place possible, and that is what the imagery seems to be trying to convey. In fact, Paul seemed to suggest as much when he wrote, "What no eye has seen, what no ear has heard, and what no human mind has conceived—the things God has prepared for those who love him" (1 Cor. 2:9). This text implies that our conceptual resources are inadequate to conceive what heaven could even be like.

Some contemporary theologians balk at the talk of heaven, worrying that too much attention has been placed on heaven and not enough on the resurrection of the body and the new creation. Moreover, some theologians are concerned that talk of heaven is too Platonic, that is, too heavily influenced by the thoughts of Plato, who seemed to believe that our souls are naturally immortal and that the body is bad. As we said before, it is difficult to know what Plato actually believed, but Christians who have talked about heaven do not believe that the body is bad but is part of God's good creation, and many Christians also believe that we are not naturally immortal—it is a supernatural act of God that keeps human beings in existence forever. Recall also that heaven is conceived as being united with God, so depending on one's theological belief about the afterlife, heaven will include both the intermediate state (if one is not in purgatory) and existence after the resurrection. So heaven is not an everlasting immaterial existence.

A major question that arises is what exactly we will be doing in heaven. Our activity can't simply be more of the same as our earthly existence. Of course we will be worshiping God. But what will that be like? Some believe that we will be so enraptured in our vision of God that we will eternally be caught up in our face-to-face union with God. That is, some theologians take a *static* view of heaven, which means that in heaven we do not undergo any changes since we will be doing one thing, which is delighting in God. This has often been referred to as the *beatific vision,* the perfect state of beatitude and joy in attaining what our hearts truly desire, which is God himself. The apostle Paul even considers our life as a race; but once you get to the finish line, you are at the end. When we see God face-to-face, we will have arrived at our final destination and the whole purpose of our lives, so why would we do anything else but worship God and enjoy being in his presence?

However, heaven is also described as a place of fellowship and communion among the saints. But it doesn't seem as though we can talk to all the saints simultaneously. Perhaps we'll spend some time dialoguing with Augustine, and then we may switch over and start asking all the questions we have for the apostle Paul. So some have adopted a *dynamic* view of heaven, in which the blessed in heaven can undergo change and engage in different activities.

Given the description of the new Jerusalem and the fact that at the resurrection we will have transformed bodies, some maintain that heaven will include many of the features of earth—so perhaps we can engage in some of the same activities, such as climbing mountains or playing musical instruments. Some theologians even posit that we might have a kind of double consciousness, where we are enjoying the beatific vision of God while we are engaged in other activities.

HEAVEN AND FREE WILL

Aside from wondering what heaven will be like and what the blessed will be doing there, some philosophical puzzles arise when thinking about heaven. One question is whether we will be free in heaven. Freedom seems to be a valuable good, but will it remain in heaven? Imagining how the blessed in heaven can have free will if there is no possibility of sinning in heaven is difficult. If we can't ever choose to perform any morally wrong action, then how could we be free in heaven?

To answer this question, we need to know what kind of freedom we are talking about. Some philosophers believe that freedom is compatible with determinism. *Determinism* is the thesis that certain conditions guarantee a single outcome. If that condition is the past and the laws of nature, then we are dealing with causal determinism. If that condition is God's foreknowledge or God's will, then we are dealing with theological determinism. So, as we discussed in chapter 2, *compatibilism* is the view that claims that freedom and determinism can go hand in hand, whereas *incompatibilism* is the view that determinism rules out freedom (and vice versa). The compatibilist has an easy answer for heavenly freedom, for even if we can never sin in heaven, we can still be free even with a single possible outcome.

But is incompatibilist freedom possible in heaven? Perhaps it can be. Some suggest that we can make choices between several goods—that is, we can choose whether to talk to Aquinas or Calvin, or to go hiking or play the guitar. But we may not have morally significant freedom, since we can never choose to sin. Others think that we might have morally significant freedom even if we can't sin, since we can choose to engage in activities that would help us grow in virtue.[13] So humans can act freely even if they can't choose to sin. Perhaps it is similar to the way that those in hell can never choose to leave, even if the option is open to them. The denizens of hell may have hardened their hearts—that is, they formed their characters in such a way as to make it psychologically impossible for them to choose otherwise. Similarly, the blessed in heaven may have formed their characters (with the help of the Holy Spirit) in such a way as to make it psychologically impossible for them to sin. That is consistent with continual growth in certain virtues as well as choosing from a range of activities (if the dynamic view is correct). So perhaps we will be free in heaven, and that may be so even if incompatibilism is true.

---

13. For more on this, see Timothy Pawl and Kevin Timpe, "Incompatibilism, Sin, and Free Will in Heaven," *Faith and Philosophy* 26 (2009): 398–419; and Pawl and Timpe, "Paradise and Growing in Virtue," in *Paradise Understood: New Philosophical Essays about Heaven*, ed. T. Ryan Byerly and Eric J. Silverman (Oxford: Oxford University Press, 2017).

HEAVEN AND ETERNAL SEPARATION

Everyone in heaven is supposed to be in a state of perfect bliss and happiness. Suppose the traditional view of hell is correct such that there are some people who will be eternally separated from God, whether because they are being punished or because they freely choose to remain in that state. But a philosophical dilemma arises: How can the blessed in heaven be perfectly happy if they know that some persons are eternally damned?

The problem is especially aggravated if the damned persons are individuals loved by the blessed in heaven. Imagine that after you die, you end up in paradise with God and the angels. But suppose you find out that someone you love—say a spouse, child, or friend—rejected God's offer of salvation and is now suffering in hell, and you also know that your loved one will experience everlasting misery. It seems that you would know the fate of your beloved; after all, Scripture even states that earthly humans have a great cloud of witnesses watching them (Heb. 12:1), which can be interpreted as including the saints in heaven. If the blessed in heaven are aware of us now, then it seems reasonable to suppose that they would be aware of the situation of others, especially those they loved in their earthly lives. Moreover, it seems that they would still love their earthly beloved. There is no marriage in heaven, but it is hard to imagine someone no longer loving their earthly spouse in heaven, even if they are no longer married. But if the lover in heaven is aware of the suffering of the beloved, it seems that the lover cannot be perfectly happy. Yet in heaven everyone is supposed to be perfectly happy. This leads to a contradiction.

Some philosophers have used this line of reasoning either to reject the traditional Christian teaching on heaven and hell (or even to reject Christianity altogether) or to support universalism—for if everyone will eventually be in heaven, then the problem of eternal separation never arises. At most, there will be temporary separation.

Christian thinkers throughout history have wrestled with this question and have offered different replies. One notable response, which often appears harsh to contemporary sensibilities, is the fact that the blessed in heaven will rejoice in their awareness of the condemnation of sinners because it manifests divine justice as well as reminds them of their fortunate position. For example, here is what the great theologian Thomas Aquinas said concerning this issue:

> The saints will rejoice in the punishment of the wicked, by considering therein the order of Divine justice and their own deliverance, which will fill them with joy. And thus the Divine justice and their own deliverance will be the direct cause of the joy of the blessed: while the punishment of the damned will cause it indirectly.[14]

Another classic example of this kind of response can be found in the works of Jonathan Edwards, who wrote,

> The saints in heaven will behold the torments of the damned. . . . Hereby the saints will be made the more sensible how great their salvation is. When they shall see how great the misery is from which God has saved them, and how great a difference he has made between their state and the state of others . . . it will give them a greater sense of the wonderfulness of God's grace to them.[15]

While the blessed in heaven may rejoice at knowing they have been saved and seeing divine justice enacted, this response misses the heart of the problem, which is the eternal separation from loved ones. So this answer provides no explanation for how heavenly saints can

---

14. Thomas Aquinas, *Summa Theologica*, Q.94, a.3, Christian Classics Ethereal Library, https://www.ccel.org/ccel/aquinas/summa.XP_Q94_A3.html.

15. Jonathan Edwards, "The Eternity of Hell Torments," *Works of Jonathan Edwards*, vol. 4, sermon 11, Christian Classics Ethereal Library, http://www.ccel.org/e/edwards/works2.iv.xii.html.

remain happy while being aware that their beloved is suffering away from them.

We believe that God will ensure that the blessed will be happy even if someone they love ends up separated from God. However, we think that God's actual ways of resolving this may be beyond our ken. Hence, we aim to provide ways God *might* do it, a way in which God allows for such separation while ensuring that he is just and that the blessed in heaven are not suffering from such separation.

One of us has opted for a position where the blessed in heaven are unaware of the condemned in hell, including those they loved in their earthly lives.[16] We can call this the *partial-amnesia solution* to the problem of eternal separation. The saints can't experience total amnesia, as that may result in a loss of personal identity or might count as harm. However, it may be that the saints in heaven are shielded from knowing what happened to their loved ones, perhaps to protect them from the pain.

But this approach raises some questions. How is the partial amnesia supposed to work? Are the memories that involve the beloved obliterated? If so, wouldn't there be strange gaps in someone's memories, especially if they knew that person for most of their lives? Or is it that only the segments in the memory are wiped? But if one's spouse is damned, does that person have a memory of standing at a wedding holding no one's hands and putting a ring on no one's finger?

In response, the partial-amnesia solution need not posit some defect or a literal loss of memory. Rather, it may be that the presence of God is so overwhelming and so captivating that those who see God face-to-face let all other concerns and thoughts fall by the wayside. Think about what happens to us when we experience something truly awesome or captivating, such as a highly improbable yet precisely executed soccer goal or the first moments of staring into the eyes of one's newborn child. We don't literally forget other things; rather, other matters fall

---

16. See chapter 7, "Heaven," in Stephen T. Davis, *After We Die: Theology, Philosophy, and the Question of Life after Death* (Waco, TX: Baylor University Press, 2015).

out of our consciousness because the current event is utterly and totally captivating. How much more will God's full presence captivate us! And so perhaps all other thoughts and concerns fall out of the consciousness of the blessed in heaven.

One of us has also proposed two underexplored responses that we think are worthy of further consideration.[17] The first approach focuses on the attribute of divine impassibility. If God is impassible, then he cannot suffer anything or be moved by anything external to God. Some take divine impassibility to imply that God has no emotions whatsoever, but a more nuanced doctrine of divine impassibility distinguishes between active emotions and passive emotions—where passive emotions have an external stimulus—and the doctrine only denies that God has the latter. Not everyone agrees that God is impassible in this way, but the dominant position throughout church history has been that God is impassible. God is aware of the vast suffering in this world, and God is also aware of those who are damned in hell, yet God's happiness is not diminished by this because God is not externally affected by such things. Some theologians have claimed that human beings become impassible in a similar manner in heaven, and so the blessed in heaven become emotionally impervious to external events, and hence they can be fully aware of the damned in hell and yet not be harmed by such knowledge since they, too, are impassible. Admittedly, it is hard to comprehend or even imagine what it would be like to be impassible or not to be subject to passions or emotions caused by external factors.

The other underexplored response is based on the concept of the *refrigerium*, which is temporary relief that some of the denizens of hell may experience. The *refrigerium* is not a part of any official teaching in Christian thought, and not many seem to endorse it. Nevertheless, a few Christian theologians do make suggestive remarks in its favor, in part because they find some intimation of a *refrigerium* in the parable

---

17. See Eric Yang, "Heaven and the Problem of Eternal Separation," in *Heaven and Philosophy*, ed. Simon Cushing (Lanham, MD: Lexington Books, 2017).

of Lazarus and the rich man in Luke 16:19–31. In that parable, Jesus depicts a rich man condemned for ignoring the plight of Lazarus. When both die, Lazarus enjoys comfort at the bosom of Abraham while the rich man experiences the agony of fiery punishment. The rich man pleads for Abraham to send Lazarus to "dip the tip of his finger in water and cool my tongue" (v. 24). On this basis, some have used this passage to suggest that there may be temporary relief for the damned in hell. Notable references to such temporary relief can be found in Augustine and C. S. Lewis. In Lewis's *The Great Divorce*, reference is made that "the damned have holidays."[18]

If we take seriously the notion of *refrigerium*, then we can see a possible answer to the problem of eternal separation. For if Lazarus could have gone down to provide some relief for the rich man, then perhaps others among the blessed might also be able to provide some relief for the denizens of hell, in particular those they loved in their earthly life. If this is right, then the solution to the problem is that there is no eternal separation, for there can be intermittent moments of union. We can compare this to someone being quarantined because they have a highly contagious disease. For the sake of society, it is good that a highly contagious person is quarantined so as not to hurt others, and hence that person must be separated. However, someone who loves the patient may visit the patient and even administer some treatment or drug to relieve the pain, or perhaps even bring over the patient's favorite food. Thus, there can be partial union between the lovers, where the lover can mitigate the suffering of the beloved.

This analogy with hell is not perfect. We might suppose those in hell deserve their punishment or have freely chosen to remain separated and have hardened their heart against God. Even so, the possibility of a *refrigerium* may enable the blessed in heaven some measure of union and a way of expressing love that mitigates the problem of eternal separation, for there can be intermittent fellowship and partial union.

---

18. C. S. Lewis, *The Great Divorce* (New York: HarperCollins, 1946), 67.

We should note that most of these responses need not be offered as ways that God will actually deal fairly with the blessed and the damned. They are what philosophers call *defenses*, ways God might do it, and that show that God is loving, just, and good even while permitting hell and separation. Thus, God's actual way of dealing fairly may be such that we can't conceive how he would do it. But the goal of philosophers has typically not been to provide that; rather, it has been the aim of showing how it is possible. Sometimes that is the most we can do through philosophical argumentation.

HEAVEN AND BOREDOM

One final issue that has often been raised in connection with heaven is its desirability. An immediate intuition and reaction seems to be that heaven and everlasting life are extremely desirable. After all, think of all the people who have searched for the fountain of youth or who strive to achieve immortality through some means. And if heaven is a place of paradise, why would someone not want to go to heaven?

But some philosophers, typically non-Christians, find heaven undesirable and claim that everlasting life would in fact be bad for humans. Perhaps the most well-known case is based on the argument that everlasting life would end up boring.[19] Take something that we enjoy doing, such as riding a favorite roller coaster or enjoying a favorite meal. Now imagine riding that roller coaster again and then again and then again and a hundred more times after that. At some point you'll get bored of that ride. Similarly, imagine eating your favorite meal, and then eating it again and again and again. At some point you'll get sick of that meal. We can extrapolate this with every possible activity. No matter how wonderful and enjoyable some event may be, after so many times, one will eventually grow tired of it. And if one lives forever, then

---

19. Bernard Williams, "The Makropulos Case: Reflections on the Tedium of Immortality," in Williams, *Problems of the Self* (Cambridge: Cambridge University Press, 1973).

one will eventually grow weary of every activity and thereby desire to no longer live—and so one is damned to everlasting boredom. This seems to be the fate of the ancient Greek gods, such as Zeus and Hera, who must endure an eternity of doing the same things over and over again, and so are hopelessly bored and miserable. This is also depicted in the story of Faust, who gets to enjoy all of the world's delights by making a bargain with the devil. But eventually he gets bored and so in the end goes with the devil.

Is there a way to stave off boredom in heaven? Perhaps the problem was thinking of doing the same thing over and over again. But activities can be pleasurable in different ways. Some pleasures are repeatable; we enjoy doing them multiple times. Other pleasures are self-exhausting; that is, once we experience them we no longer have a desire for more of the same. Examples of repeatable pleasures are fine dining or reading one's favorite book. Examples of self-exhausting pleasures may be (depending on your desires) being the first to climb a certain mountain or graduating high school. Perhaps boredom can be avoided if an immortal person spends some time engaged in a package of repeatable pleasures and then rotates various packages of repeatable pleasures.[20] That is, she may spend the first fifty years learning some musical instruments, cooking and eating Italian and Japanese dishes, and mastering chess. After that, she may spend the next fifty years getting better at her soccer skills, learning various forms of dance, and learning to speak three languages. And she can continue to rotate these pleasures along with other valuable endeavors. So after many years of not eating a certain dish, she may come back to that dish and be surprised by how good it tastes. Thus, boredom may be thwarted.

That said, perhaps one might get bored not just of specific activities but also by *types* of activities, and so the threat of boredom may not be entirely eliminated. However, many Christian thinkers believe that the reason boredom will not occur is because we cannot yet imagine

---

20. For more on this response, see John Martin Fischer, "Why Immortality Is Not So Bad," *International Journal of Philosophical Studies* 2 (1994): 257–70.

how great the good of heaven truly is. The beatific vision—seeing God face-to-face—is utterly incomprehensible to us right now. How do you imagine something that no eye has seen and no ear has heard, and that has not entered into the mind of human beings (1 Cor. 2:9)? For Christian thinkers, the worry of boredom is not too disconcerting since there is already an admission of a certain ignorance of what heaven will be like. In this way the static conception of heaven may be deemed as more plausible than previously thought. The dynamic conception seems attractive given that we currently enjoy a plethora of activities. But these are all finite activities that could lead to eventual boredom. But if the greatest good is perfect union with God, then perhaps we won't have desires for any other activities. Again, this doesn't rule out the dynamic conception, but the static conception does merit some serious consideration, especially if we are willing to admit that we cannot apprehend the goodness of what is to come in heaven.

CONCLUDING THOUGHTS

For Christians, heaven is not merely theoretical—it is our hope and our ultimate home, to be with God forever. For many, it constitutes a significant part of an answer to suffering (Rom. 8:18). Heaven is not an escape but a redemption of the suffering that humans face. Heaven also declares the victory of God, that despite appearances to the contrary, justice will prevail. Though injustices are rampant and widespread, and though the righteous suffer and the wicked prosper, this will not always be so. Justice will be done, and heaven declares that God's victory is decisive even now. Heaven, then, is our hearts' desire, since our hearts' ultimate desire is union with God. For those who entrust themselves to God through the redemptive work of Christ, they will see and receive what they have been wanting all along.

So it is important to remember not to lose sight of the true value of heaven. But this doesn't mean we can't or shouldn't ask questions about heaven. Several questions naturally arise, and we have asked them and examined several answers to these questions. We often have many questions for things we dread and things we are excited for, especially if there is much we do not understand. Before a surgical procedure, we may ask many questions out of fear or anxiety. Before going to a theme park, children will ask hundreds of questions out of excitement. So it is no surprise that Christians have had questions about hell and heaven. This is part of the enterprise of faith seeking understanding.

FURTHER READINGS

For an overview of many of the themes discussed in this chapter, see Stephen T. Davis, *After We Die: Theology, Philosophy, and the Question of Life after Death* (Waco, TX: Baylor University Press, 2015). For an excellent treatment of many of the philosophical issues pertaining to hell, heaven, and purgatory, we recommend the trilogy by Jerry Walls: *Hell: The Logic of Damnation* (Notre Dame, IN: University of Notre Dame Press, 1992), *Heaven: The Logic of Eternal Joy* (Oxford: Oxford University Press, 2002), and *Purgatory: The Logic of Total Transformation* (Oxford: Oxford University Press, 2011). For an extended defense of universalism, see Thomas Talbott, *The Inescapable Love of God* (Eugene, OR: Cascade Books, 2014). Two recent volumes discuss many of the issues covered in this chapter that pertain to heaven: T. Ryan Byerly and Eric J. Silverman, *Paradise Understood: New Philosophical Essays about Heaven* (Oxford: Oxford University Press, 2017), and Simon Cushing, *Heaven and Philosophy* (Lanham, MD: Lexington Books, 2017).

ADDITIONAL THEOLOGICAL ISSUES

In this final chapter, we want to briefly present some of the current work in contemporary philosophical theology concerning other doctrines of great importance to Christians. Hopefully you'll get a sense of some of the issues and various positions, and you might want to think through some of these topics for yourself.

ASCENSION

Scripture says that Christ ascended into heaven and is now seated at the right hand of the Father (Luke 24:50–53, Acts 1:1–11). And the Apostles' Creed states that Christ "ascended into heaven and is seated at the right hand of the Father." This language of being seated at the right hand of the Father is clearly figurative, especially since the Father, being wholly immaterial, doesn't literally have a right hand. Rather, the phrase, "being at the right hand," was commonly used to express power and authority. However, the ascension is usually meant to imply that Christ retained his human nature, soul and body.

So how should we understand the ascension? Some people may even be embarrassed by the teaching, since it may lead them to think that Jesus is flying around in space! However, many take seriously the metaphorical language, especially the symbolic role that clouds play as indicating the presence of God (see, e.g., Ex. 19:9; Dan. 7:13; Mark 9:7). Hence, the key point of the passages representing the ascension is that Jesus passed from the presence of the disciples into the presence of God.

But several philosophical questions naturally arise. Christ retained his body, and if Elijah and Enoch were bodily assumed into heaven, then they, too, would presumably still have their bodies in heaven, but how is that supposed to work? Recall that in chapter 7 we allowed the term *heaven* to mean any place where one is in the full presence of God, whether that is the intermediate state or the post-resurrection state. But given that the resurrection has not yet occurred, can there be bodies in the intermediate state? And if so, where are they? Are they in our space-time universe or some other spatiotemporal domain? Is there a space-like or physical-like quality to heaven, even during the intermediate state? Some philosophers have found philosophical and scientific discussion of space and time useful here, especially perhaps the concept of passing from one space-time manifold into another. So perhaps the intermediate state should not be construed as purely immaterial but as partly physical (or physical-like) and partly immaterial.

ORIGINAL SIN

Many Western Christians believe that because of the fall (that is, the first sin of the first human beings), all humans have what is known as *original sin*. The doctrine of original sin traditionally includes the affirmations that (1) human beings are all guilty before God at the moment we come into existence, (2) human beings all have a strong inclination to sin, and (3) human beings will all sin at least once in our lives, though likely we will sin many more times than that.

A philosophical conundrum arises over the doctrine of original sin that has to do with (1): How is it possible to be guilty for something that we didn't do? If you rob a bank, it would be unjust to punish someone else for the crime. Similarly, the first human beings sinned a long time ago and in a faraway place, and it may seem unfair that we are all guilty for their sin, especially since it appears that there is nothing we could have done about it. So how could we be guilty or held responsible for something that we could have done nothing about or did not have under our control?

Because of this seeming injustice, some Christian philosophers reject (1) and accept only (2) and (3) in the doctrine of original sin. However, other Christian philosophers have defended (1). Some suggest that there is a kind of representation (a "federal headship") that the first humans had by which the rest of us are guilty—perhaps the way a debt can be passed down from parent to progeny. This response seems popular among Reformed thinkers, especially for those who take seriously the concept of the imputation of guilt.

Others argue for a more philosophically complex approach, that we have a *temporal stage* that we share with the first human who fell, or that we have *counterfactual power* over whether the first humans would fall or not.[1] It is evident, then, that the acceptance of (1) is not a simple issue but requires some deep reflection.

Other philosophers have been concerned over (2). Why is there this new inclination to sin, and what does that mean regarding human nature? Has our nature changed—and will our nature change again in heaven? And what exactly happens in that change? Did we gain something or lose something? Some Christian philosophers think that we lost something in the fall. For example, Anselm believed that humans lost God's justice, which was originally a part of us. Others think we gained something, like contracting a disease or an infection, which can then be passed on to descendants (and some medieval theologians believed that it was passed on biologically, much like a genetic disease). So, which is it more like—did human nature gain something or lose something at the fall?

---

1. For more on both of these approaches, see Michael Rea, "The Metaphysics of Original Sin," in *Persons: Human and Divine*, ed. Peter van Inwagen and Dean Zimmerman (Oxford: Oxford University Press, 2007).

PETITIONARY PRAYER

Another topic that has intrigued Christian philosophers for some time is the notion of petitionary prayer. There are many different forms of prayer, such as thanksgiving and adoration, but God has commanded that we ask him for things, most clearly in the Lord's Prayer ("Give us this day our daily bread"). So making requests to God is a regular part of Christian practice. Many Christians also believe that God sometimes answers prayers. But what is it for God to answer prayers? A naive answer is that you ask God for something, and then it happens, and therefore you conclude that God answered it. But this can't be right, for it commits the fallacy known as *post hoc ergo propter hoc*, "after this, therefore because of this." That is, just because *a* happens before *b* does not guarantee that *a* is what brings about *b*. Simply by praying for something to happen and then it happens doesn't guarantee that it is an answer to prayer, for it may be a mere coincidence. After all, God might have already planned on bringing that event about even if you didn't pray for it. Or it seems that a person can ask for some horrible thing to befall an innocent individual, and then it happens, but many theologians believe that God does not answer such wicked prayers.

A more common way of analyzing answered prayer is to put it in a conditional with a subjunctive mood (that is, in a "If . . . then . . . would . . ." statement). That is, God answers someone's prayer for something to happen just in case it wouldn't have happened if that person hadn't prayed for it to happen. So, suppose Peter prays that God will restore his hand, and his hand is restored. However, suppose that had Peter not prayed, his hand would not have been restored. Then we can say that God answered his prayer. While this sophisticated model is a bit more nuanced than the naive position, it, too, seems to be unsatisfactory. Imagine you and Clara pray for someone to be healed. It may be the case that if you had not prayed for it, God still would have brought about the healing on the basis of Clara's prayer. But if this is right, then by the previous analysis, God doesn't answer your prayer since he would have done it anyway even if you hadn't prayed. So that theory of answered prayer must not be correct. It should be evident that coming up with an analysis of answered prayer is quite difficult. It seems that we should say that your prayer for a particular thing to happen is a reason why God brings about the event that you are asking for, but it is hard to specify exactly how that should be formulated.[2]

Another philosophical puzzle asks whether it even makes sense for humans to offer petitionary prayers. If God is omniscient (God knows everything there is to know) and wholly good, then God already knows what we need and plans to give what is best for us. So why bother with asking God if God already knows what he plans to do? It seems that our prayers wouldn't be effective; after all, we're not going to give better advice to God! Some concede and claim that our prayers are not effective: they don't change or influence God's mind at all. According to this view, the same outcome would have happened whether we prayed or not.

Other Christian philosophers defend the claim that God is responsive to our prayers, and so our prayers can be effective, but making such a claim may affect our concept of God. One issue is whether God can be responsive to our prayers while also being unchanging or impassible, which are traditional attributes of God. Some philosophers think that God's responsiveness implies that God cannot be timeless or exist outside of time but rather must exist in time in order to answer prayers. To say that God is in time is to say that God experiences events successively (that is, one after the other) just like we do. However, other Christian philosophers argue that God's responsiveness to our prayers is compatible with the attributes of divine immutability and timelessness.

Another puzzle surrounds knowing whether an event occurred because you prayed for it or because God already had some prior reason for bringing about that event. Short of a miracle, it appears

---

2. For an excellent discussion on these issues, see Scott Davison, *Petitionary Prayer* (Oxford: Oxford University Press, 2017).

quite difficult to know whether God would have brought about your request independent of your asking, or whether God did so because you asked. This question is different because it doesn't claim that God doesn't answer your prayer; rather, it shows the potential intellectual limitations we have in our ability to determine whether a prayer was actually answered or not.

C. S. Lewis also raised a similar worry because of the fact that Scripture yields two putatively conflicting models of prayer.[3] One model of prayer implies asking with strong faith and certitude. For example, in Matthew 21:21–22 Jesus said, "You can say to this mountain, 'Go, throw yourself into the sea,' and it will be done. If you believe, you will receive whatever you ask for in prayer." However, in Matthew 26:39 Jesus said, "My Father, if it is possible, may this cup be taken from me. Yet not as I will, but as you will." This model of prayer exhibits a submissive attitude. Lewis worried how one could psychologically hold both attitudes simultaneously, and so the question is which attitude one should have when praying. Lewis never seemed to provide an answer to his concern but only noted the puzzle of both models being found in Scripture.

SOME REMAINING ISSUES

Many other topics in Christian theology have drawn the attention of contemporary Christian philosophers. Some philosophers have discussed issues pertaining to liturgy, ecclesiology, pneumatology, and sacramental theology. Others have paid a good deal of attention to the theological virtues of faith, hope, and love. For example, we can ask whether faith includes belief. If so, is it just belief, or does it involve belief plus something else—and if the latter, what is that something else? Does it require trust? Perhaps faith doesn't include belief, but

---

3. C. S. Lewis, "Petitionary Prayer: A Problem without an Answer," in *The Seeing Eye*, ed. Walter Hooper (New York: Ballantine Books, 1967).

only acting as if the claims were true? And what is the relation of faith to evidence and reason? Is faith opposed to objective reason and evidence (in a way that Søren Kierkegaard seemed to suggest), or does faith presuppose reason and evidence (in a way that Aquinas seemed to suggest)? And can one have faith while they are in heaven, or does one lose faith in heaven now that it has become sight?

Philosophical theology, then, is not constrained to any particular set of topics—it is merely employing the rigorous tools of philosophical thinking (making arguments, defining terms precisely, making clear distinctions, etc.) to what has been revealed to us by God. Unlike the project of natural theology, we are not trying to find reasons for believing in these claims. Rather, we are trying to understand what it is that we believe, to broaden our appreciation and knowledge of God and what God has done for us.

FURTHER READINGS

For some philosophical discussion of the ascension, see the chapter "Ascension and the Second Coming" in Stephen T. Davis, *After We Die* (Waco, TX: Baylor University Press, 2015). For some recent work on original sin, see Michael Rea, "The Metaphysics of Original Sin," in *Persons: Human and Divine*, ed. Peter van Inwagen and Dean Zimmerman (Oxford: Oxford University Press, 2007); and Oliver Crisp, *Jonathan Edwards and the Metaphysics of Sin* (New York: Routledge, 2005). On petitionary prayer, an excellent overview and novel lines of inquiry can be found in Scott Davison, *Petitionary Prayer: A Philosophical Investigation* (Oxford: Oxford University Press, 2017). For recent work on faith, see Laura Frances Callahan and Timothy O'Connor, *Religious Faith and Intellectual Virtue* (Oxford: Oxford University Press, 2014).

AFTERWORD

We hope that in reading this book you found plenty to think about and to challenge the depth and breadth of your understanding of core Christian doctrines. If you are walking away with more questions than answers, then we are with you. Although we have taken a stance on some of these issues (and the two of us do not always agree), we recognize how tentative some of these views and conclusions are, but perhaps that is how it should be for those who recognize their own cognitive limitations and fallibility. Thanks be to God that he has provided for us the revelation that we need for our salvation, and a graduate degree in philosophy or theology is not required to understand that. But as we have been reiterating throughout, we believe that faith seeks understanding, because a lover desires to know as much as possible about the beloved. We want to know and love God the best we can. Even though we are academics, we do not think that reflecting on these theological topics is merely an academic game. We want to know and love God because we believe these are the central reasons why we exist.

We also hope that you do not walk away from having read this book discouraged. There is so much to learn, and we have so little time. As the author of Ecclesiastes reminds us, "Of making many books there is no end, and much study wearies the body" (Eccl. 12:12). There are also no easy answers to these difficult questions. But we have been commanded to love God with our minds (Luke 10:27).

We hope that this book has provided a useful introduction for those of you who have the desire to study some of these topics in further depth. It is unlikely that one person can master all of these topics, but hopefully you now have a better grasp of the theological issues that Christian thinkers have been wrestling with throughout history and up to the present. What is currently pressing is the need for integrating the different theological disciplines. So those with an expertise in biblical exegesis, historical theology, or systematic theology would do well to integrate some of the arguments and views from philosophical theology into these disciplines, as well as to offer constructive criticisms to philosophers and analytic theologians.

Although not everyone reading this book will be an academic, we are convinced that every Christian has much to contribute to the discussion. We also believe that Christian philosophers have much to contribute to the discussion, and so we wrote this book with the hope that Christians will see the benefit of employing the logical tools and the conceptual resources that come from historical and contemporary philosophical theologians. But so much more is involved in theology. Narrative, imagination, personal experience, discussion, prayer, spiritual discipline, the hearing of Scripture, and so much more can help us in our understanding of the Christian faith.

We desire for the church to be united in all of its endeavors, for example, caring for the poor and sick as well as understanding the God who has revealed himself to us. And so we encourage students, seminarians, pastors, church leaders, and faithful church members to start dialoguing about these issues. As you study these topics, you should be asking yourself how your own view fits with Scripture and whether the view is coherent or intelligible. Both of us can attest to how much we have learned from those outside of academia, especially those who are thoughtful and careful when thinking about Christian theology. So we hope that Christians of all stripes will take part in our task of faith seeking understanding.

INDEX

An Introduction to Christian Philosophical Theology Video Lectures

Stephen T. Davis and Eric T. Yang

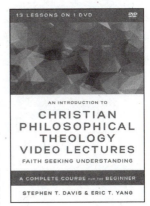

Philosophical or analytic theology seeks to employ philosophical tools while studying topics in Christian theology and examining the logical consistency or intelligibility of some of the key doctrines of the Christian faith. In this accessible introduction, *An Introduction to Christian Philosophical Theology Video Lectures*, Stephen T. Davis and Eric T. Yang first explain the scope, relevance, and value of philosophical theology and then apply its conceptual tools to examine each of the core Christian doctrines:

- Revelation and Scripture
- The Trinity
- The incarnation
- Redemption and the atonement,
- Resurrection and life after death

The final session briefly addresses some additional theological issues including petitionary prayer, eschatology, and original sin.

Designed for beginning students and nonspecialists, this guide provides the ideal entry point for understanding not only what philosophical theology is but also how it can provide valuable insights for how we think about the core doctrines of the Christian faith.

Available in stores and online!